THE THICK BLUE LINE

(One story of policing 1963 – 1981)

by

Ian Patterson

Illustrations by
John Patterson

Acknowledgements

The author would like to thank Harry Wright, retired superintendent of the Worcestershire and West Mercia Constabularies, Denis Powell, retired detective constable of the Hereford and West Mercia forces and Tommy Charlton, retired chief inspector of the West Riding of Yorkshire and Northumberland police for their help and support. A special thanks to Tommy for the title idea.

The names and locations mentioned in the book have been changed to avoid embarrassment.

In fact, do you remember an American television programme from many years ago? I think it was called 'The Naked City.' At the end of each episode someone would say something like, "There a ten thousand stories in the Naked City. This has been one of them." Well, there are quite a few little stories here - only I'm going to leave you to judge which are100% true and which have been 'gilded' a little.

Published by GET Publishing, 57 Queens Road, Bridgnorth, Shropshire WV15 5DG
info@getpublishing.co.uk

ISBN 978-0-9548793-2-5

Printed in the United Kingdom by Hobbs the Printers Ltd., Brunel Road, Totton, Hampsire SO40 3WX

*****

A scientist, an artist and a policeman are set a task. Each is given two small ball bearings and told they have a week to come up with something appertaining to their own particular field of expertise. To aid concentration, each is locked in a separate room.

After the week has passed the scientist is asked, "What have you done with your ball bearings?"

"I've designed an experiment whereby if the balls are struck together in a certain way, I can measure and deduce and prove how light travels through the universe."

Fantastic!

Next, the artist is asked the same question and he produces one ball bearing sitting on top of the other, the uppermost having being minutely carved into the shape of palm fronds.

"Fantastic! Well done!"

In the last room is the policeman. He is found sitting in the corner with his head in his hands rocking too and fro.

"What's the matter with you?" he's asked.

"Nuthin!" comes the surly reply.

"Well, what have you managed to produce with the two ball bearings that I left you with?"

"Nuthin!"

"That's most disappointing. What happened?"

"Lost one and broke the other."

Welcome to The Thick Blue Line!

*****

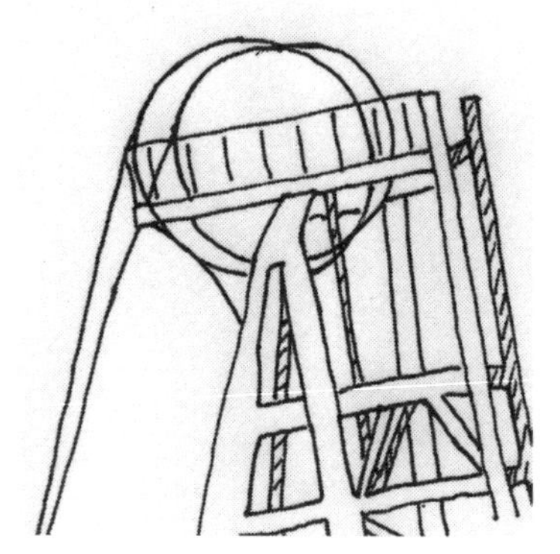

YORKSHIRE
1963 - 1970

*****

INTRODUCTION

Has anyone been 'in-bye?'

You know – plummet down a mine shaft in a metal cage for a mile or so beneath the earth and then trudge and scramble toward the ever increasing, Banshee-like noise of tortured machinery attacking a wall of coal hidden in the far blackness.

For over two hundred years, generation after generation of my family were coal miners on the Northumberland, Durham and Yorkshire coalfields. They eked out a living, facing death and injury on a daily basis – and kept doing it. No mystery as to the 'why.' Put simply, they didn't have a choice.

But I did. One trip 'in-bye' to experience the nearest thing to hell-on-earth was enough. I needed a life elsewhere.

But where? The choices for a fifteen year old clutching a school leaving certificate signed by the headmaster, (Ian will surprise us all one day,) were somewhat limited in a Northumbrian pit village.

The family were pleased I wangled a job in the Trade Union office. Then not so pleased when I left for Yorkshire and a career in the police – the auld enemy of class struggle. Still, they had to admit a regular wage and a pension at the end of it was an attractive alternative to their life of uncertainty and hardship.

So, I boarded the steam train for Yorkshire – change at York for Leeds, (you can't get lost if you've a tongue in your head,) – with the words of my grandma ringing in my ears: "Just promise me, son. You won't vote Tory."

So I swapped a pit village for a typical, mucky mill town in the West Riding.

The first thing which met me from the bus window was – wait for it – rhubarb! Fields of the stuff. At home everyone grew it, only there it was in little clumps at the bottom of the garden near the outside loo. Not so in this part of Yorkshire. It had to be the rhubarb capital of the world. They say it thrives on muck – and this particular mill town did nothing to disprove that statement.

The bus sped on; gasworks, tanneries, oil depots, dyers, sewage works, abattoirs, meat canning factories. But most of all, woollen mills. Huge, square and sturdy buildings, somehow reflecting the values of their Victorian founders. These fortresses certainly dominated the town, and being so high they made it impossible for sunlight to reach the people hurrying about their business below. But it was the smell I remember. Not the crashing, rackety-clackety noise of the looms which filtered into the streets, but the smell of hot oil and damp wool. It was as if it had been trapped in those canyons for a hundred years. It literally turned your stomach.

The bus deposited me and my granddad's battered suitcase outside the grandiose town hall. A once white, builders van with ladders sticking out the back flashed passed. All I could see of the driver was a yellow turban – something I'd not seen before. On the vans side: 'You've tried the cowboys. Now try the Indians. Phone –.'

My smile didn't last long. I looked left and right along the single main street, wondered at the ankle deep litter blowing every which way, [within days you never even noticed it,] before deciding I'd better find the police station.

It was 4 p.m. and already getting dark. And it was a week before Christmas, 1963.

I was cold, damp and frightened half to death. To make matters worse, I couldn't stop thinking about the young man arriving with me for our first day at the initial police training establishment of Panel Ash, just outside Harrogate. He was lugging two heavy suitcases up the long drive and making heavy weather of it. The drill sergeant bawling and shouting at him didn't help matters. He called the new recruit every name under the sun – and then some, until the lad, [no one ever knew his name,] put down both cases, turned himself around, picked up his luggage and headed for home. He was never seen again.

I now knew how he felt. But for me anything, no matter how strange, was better than the alternative: The Pit!

THE ARRIVAL

The police station I came to love was a strange place, hidden away as it was deep in the bowels of the very grand Victorian town hall. Like the edifice above, the 'nick' was solid, built to last, with no time for frills or frippery.

Access for everyone - members of the public, police officers, prisoners, new fresh faced constables in ill-fitting suits – was down a flight of fifteen stone steps. These were well worn after a century of constant comings and goings.

Once inside, the long, tiled and darkened corridor resounded with the sounds of leather soles, clashing doors and the laboured striking of typewriter keys. So intermittent was the sound of the single, distant typewriter, it was easy to imagine much silent swearing as the officer concentrated on using his circular typewriter rubber, trying [in vain] not to mess up the carbon copies.

To the left of the stairs lay the main office with its Olympic-like coal fire. It never went out, summer or winter. The place was too old and too draughty – even without windows.

And behind the cosy office smelling of polish, cigarette smoke, soot and fried food, lay the cells. Dungeons would be a better description and surely they must have been the best crime prevention method ever devised. One night in there with the sordid smells and the sounds of rats running the heating pipes, would make a coal miner of anyone.

To the right of the entrance stairs lay the long, dark corridor. I later discovered it led to a number of small rooms; the C.I.D., canteen-cum-briefing room, etc., and an internal staircase leading to the haughty Magistrates' Court and the equally fearful office of the unapproachable, god-like figure of the Inspector. You just didn't want to go up those stairs even it meant seeing daylight for a while. [The Inspector's office was the only room in the police station with natural light.]

But all that was for the future. For now, a deep breath and an over-loud knock on the small, opaque window of the office which brought forth the first encounter with my sergeant to be. He was short for a policeman, maybe five feet nine tall, but with bull shoulders. His hair was close cropped and dark; his eyes as hard as flint.

He almost broke my hand with his handshake as he introduced himself. "I'm Sergeant Keating." His eyes looked me up and down, taking his time to study this apparition before him. I could hear him saying to himself, 'For * sake! What have they sent me now?'

I tried to look back at him with a confidence I didn't feel. The first minute of my first day and not even shaving yet, [well, I'd tried it once and didn't like it so gave it up,] and, "I'm Sergeant Patterson," I replied.

His face said it all. 'I'm going to have to keep an eye on this one.'

"You can start by getting the coal buckets filled. Then stoke the Inspector's fire while I sort your digs out," he ordered.

Two hours later and I knew my lodgings were going to be nothing like my mum's place. For one thing, we may have been poor, but there were never little mounds of dog turd on the front room floor – nor, come to think of it – a drunken labourer lying half on and half off 'my' bed.

One thing was for sure. I'd have to find somewhere else to stay if I was going to stand a chance of seeing through my two year probationary period.

THE PIGEON

Well, I was right about Sergeant 'Rip' Keating. He wasn't sure about his new acquisition at all. And when he wasn't sure about someone – or if that someone crossed him – he had his own methods of discipline.

I swear this wasn't my fault. Imagine… First full day and I'm stoking the office fire [again] when a gentleman knocks on the enquiry hatch. He hands me a cardboard box containing a pigeon. Not any old bird of course, but a racing pigeon complete with a ring on one of its very valuable legs.

A call to someone who knew about such things revealed it was a prize winner, the father of many and it had got lost somewhere over Castleford three days earlier. And yes – the owner would hot-foot over just as soon as his shift was finished.

To keep the thing safe, I thought it would be a good idea to put it in the stray dog pound out the back. A dark kennel would be just the thing to reduce stress and aid recovery. So that's what happened.

By 5 p.m. I was heading for tea when a bedraggled mongrel was being left with another hapless policeman who had better things to do. He did the paperwork before pushing the half-starved beast into the pound. No dog food – it wasn't provided in those days – and the constable had no intention of handing over his cheese sarnies.

And that was that – until the pigeon's owner turned up pleased that his prize bird had been found and was in safe hands. He was so excited he was bobbing up and down.

But that didn't last long. He left distressed – his bird had somehow found a hole in the wire mesh and flown off. He wasn't to know that it must have been a very small hole – what with the hundreds of feathers it left behind.

Mind you, the scruffy hound didn't seem to mind being on its own. It was licking its lips and grinning hugely.

The punishment! Churwell Hill! Now, back in the early sixties there was no such things as radios for foot constables. We had to make 'points' at appointed times, [arrive five minutes before and remain until five minutes after the set time] at either one of the old, square police boxes so beloved by Doctor Who, or more normally, at telephone kiosks. Being given half hour points, meant you had twenty minutes to make the mile down Churwell Hill to the kiosk there – then twenty minutes to haul yourself back up the long incline. The offending officers – in this case the one who hadn't fed the dog and me, Pigeon Boy – passed one another at a near trot without the oxygen necessary for small talk.

Repeat for eight hours. [And woe-betide you if you're late!]

KUNG-FU FIGHTING

But things improved quite quickly.

Sergeant Keating accompanied me on my first Saturday night patrol as the pubs kicked out at 10.30 p.m. It was somewhat reassuring to know I was in good hands [large and gnarled] as Rip had been the British Army on the Rhine boxing champion for several years during a previous life.

We were standing at the kerb edge near the town hall when a pimply youth approached, obviously well under the influence of drink. Rather than being noisy or boisterous or downright objectionable to all about him, he fancied himself as a martial arts expert. One leg would rise to knee height – then he'd stagger. He cut the air with the edges of his hands

– very slow chopping movements. And that was okay until he approached first me, then Rip.

I blinked as the chopping motion stopped an inch from my nose.

"Go home, lad!" suggested the Sergeant.

The youth didn't hear the menace carried in the voice and moved from me to confront the speaker. A couple more Kung-Fu moves!

"Last chance, son. Go home!"

Another chopping motion toward Sergeant Keating's face!

I understood everything right there and then. First - how Rip had been a champion. His uppercut travelled no more than six inches. In itself, the blow would have felled most assailants, but the elbow following through and connecting with the jaw for a second helping, was pure class. The lad went down – down into the gutter and stayed there.

Without more ado, the sergeant stepped over the prostrate figure and meandered off. I followed, now understanding something else as well. Should a complaint ever be made, I'd agree with whatever the sergeant decided was the truth.

THREE FOR THE PRICE OF ONE

Shortly afterwards I was sent off on my own. Twenty minutes after midnight and I was ambling down the steep incline of the main street toward an unpleasant area of town called 'The Bottoms.' It was well named – the night hours saw it frequented by the flotsam and jetsam of society. Or to put it another way, you wouldn't ask any of the folk found around there after midnight round to your place for a cup of tea.

And from the noise in the distance it was obvious even to me that a fight was in progress. Long after closing hours, a local publican had eventually thrown out his recalcitrant drinkers who then responded in time honoured fashion.

I have to admit that I considered doing an about-turn. Then I thought of Sergeant Rip's displeasure, a return to the dole queue or the beckoning pit. Moments later, I waded in.

"Break it up! Break it up! Show some respect for the Queen's uniform!"

And it worked.

There were three main offenders and it didn't take my school leaving certificate in arithmetic, [c- if you must know,] to work out one drunk in each hand leaves one drunk spare.

"You! Follow me!"

And he did - all the way to the police station. On arrival, I briefed Sergeant Keating as to the circumstances of the arrests.

His reply was a little disconcerting. "Ian! You're going to have to slow down a bit. You've been here three days and I've not understood a word you've said yet."

Just for the briefest of moments the sergeant's eye held the first glimmer of hope for my fledgling career.

BASSA AND THE GYPSY

It was just as well I'd made my first arrest - the three drunks - and on my own, because things got a little strained a few days later.

It was an afternoon shift, [2pm – 10pm] and I was under the supervision of a florid-faced constable called 'Bassa.' He was a real old timer with bulging silver buttons across an ample belly and a generous moustache full of odd bits and pieces of left over food.

We were briefed at 1.45 p.m. and told to be on the look-out for a gypsy type complete with ear-rings and tattoos. If that wasn't enough he'd have a black and white horse with him which was old enough to have been at Waterloo. The horse was attached to a cart laden with lead stolen from a church roof.

To avoid work, Bassa led me down to the canal towpath – only to find our way blocked by – you guessed it. Bassa was very good about it. He let me talk to the gypsy type whilst he climbed up onto the cart and ferreted about looking for the lead.

I passed the time by doing policeman-like stuff:

"Name!"

"O'Royan, sur."

"Address!"

"Now then sur, you got me there. Tell you what, could ye be an angel of mercy and just hang on ti' this 'orse o' mine. I just need to take a …… - to relieve mysel' ower there."

He handed over the horse reins so forcefully that I took them without a murmur.

The gypsy man certainly 'went over there.' Unfortunately, he was travelling at the speed of light and was never to be seen again.

Bassa's punishment to me: to lead the horse and cart back to the police station through the town centre. With everyone staring at you, it's really belittling.

Sergeant Keating's punishment: daily shifts that went 10 a.m. – 2 p.m. 10 p.m. – 2 a.m. for what seemed like an eternity. That's quite tiring too.

Redemption was a long time coming and took three forms:

Electric Dogs

I got to kill the stray dogs. Horrific but true. The unfortunate creatures had seven days from the time they were handed in for someone to claim them – then they were destroyed. That sounds a lot more civilized than the actuality: Lead the animals onto a metal tray covered in water and throw the switch.

But that's the truth of what used to happen. The sergeants all held the same opinion – it was character building for the young officers.

My First Road Traffic Accident

The second step on the path to redemption involved my first ever road traffic accident. And of course it wasn't a nice, simple minor collision.

During the three month long initial training period, new constables spent a lot of time learning their powers, i.e. what they could lawfully do once they were let out onto the unsuspecting public. This was done endlessly and 'parrot-fashion.' And one of the worst powers – if not the longest, certainly the most complicated - was the one involving a horse being injured in a road accident where it needed putting out of its misery and where the owner was not present.

It was a nightmare on paper, a nightmare in the examinations and a whole lot worse when it happens in reality. And guess what….. A gypsy horse had managed to escape from its tether on the verge of the main road to Leeds and decided to go walk-about amongst the lorries. The inevitable happened – both to the horse and the constable on duty. Me!

But I got it right, a pocket note book full of the correct signatures and procedures which brought a grin to the sergeant's face. That was something worth more than gold.

Constable Scarborough

But the biggest single factor in my redemption from Mr O'Royan's horse and cart was the arrival of Police Constable Joseph Scarborough. He became a legend within days and gave us all a respite from the wrath which seemed to perpetually surround us.

Joe was big. He was six feet four inches tall and his towering frame would best be described as 'ample.' He had to go through the doors in the police station sideways. For sure the Army would never have taken him – he was too unfit. And no career involving apprenticeships to electricians, plumbers, plasterers, etc. would ever open their doors to him – for poor Joe was as thick as a plank. So really, the police was an ideal career for him.

Can't you just feel a 'but' coming on. It may be a little thing, but Joe was frightened of the dark. Not just wary of it, but he had the real gut-wrenching fear of sweaty nightmares.

And could he sweat! From the moment he donned his night helmet – the one with the black badge instead of the shiny silver one – the sweat began. Rivers of it! Now, Police Constable Scarborough wasn't a good looking brute at the best of times, his features being dominated by a large, hooked predatory nose from which the sweat streamed continuously.

It transformed him from a figure of authority to one of derision. Not that the derision came from his colleagues – we actually liked him and felt sorry for him. But we could do nothing about the derision he received on the street. That was something else.

To make matters worse, the station began receiving phone calls in the dead of night by irate, would-be slumberers. The gist of their complaints was that a man in a top hat was singing at the top of his voice. He was walking down the middle of the road flashing a torch this way and that. Night after night the phone calls continued, until the Inspector began asking questions.

It was Joe, of course. But no one snitched. We organized it so, where possible, he could walk alongside night shift workers heading for the bus depot or railway sidings. We even endorsed the telephone message pads with a variety of 'results.'

I'm sure Sergeant Keating knew - nothing got passed him - and there couldn't be that many fancy dress parties taking place in a mill town every night of the week. Well, on the nights our 'B' shift was out and about.

THE INSPECTOR

But no one could save poor Constable Scarborough from Inspector William M. Masterton.

I'd thought Sergeant Keating was a hard man, but he paled into insignificance in the presence of the inspector. It was strange how the two smallest men in the station could dominate the huge officers under their command, but they did. And it wasn't only the men. They dominated 'their' streets to.

But it was Inspector Masterton who ruled the roost. He ruled with a rod of iron, marching stick under one arm, slashed peaked cap, shiny black Oxford shoes and a uniform pressed to within an inch of its life. Man management was an unknown concept to him – you just did your job or accept the consequences.

And one day I witnessed his wrath at first hand.

We'd had a shop broken into overnight, not an unknown occurrence, but unusual. And this shop just happened to be situated on the main street of the town. In fact, the broken window in the front door should have been found by the patrolling night shift officers had they been shaking hands with the door knobs as they were supposed to in the wee, small hours. [Property had to be physically checked, back and front, once before the foot patrols meal break and once after.] Obviously someone hadn't been doing their job.

As it happened the break-in couldn't have come at a worse time. On a neighbouring city sub-division a joke was doing its rounds: 'Lend 'is a fag 'til the shops shut.' Only it was no joke. A night shift was plundering fags from shops and selling them around the working men's clubs.

And that was not going to happen on Masterton's Watch. Not if the Inspector had anything to do with it. Whilst the offending night shift officers were being turned out of their beds after three hours sleep, the inspector ordered a telephone call to the Chief Constable at headquarters. A bit of reassurance to those on high was in order. Then he waited.

Unbeknownst to him, in the subterranean world far below, Police Constable Joseph Scarborough was manning the switchboard – one of those pre-war, A1 London contraptions with a hundred holes and dual connecting leads and flaps and a handle to ring the required extension. Everyone hated it.

The telephone rang in Masterton's sunlit office. It was the Chief Constable at last. "Good morning, Sir," the inspector began politely.

"Is that you Masters?" [The Chief wasn't good with names.]

"Masterton, Sir," the inspector corrected. Then…..Buzzzzz.

He'd been cut off. Within seconds, he burst into the front office. He was beyond annoyed. The familiar red face was long gone. He was deathly pale. And trembling, his eyes filled with cold fury. I sank behind the large, leather bound, gold lettered occurrence book, not daring to breathe. But it wasn't me – it was Joe he sought out.

And just as the inspector stormed in, the A1 telephone system lit up like a Christmas tree accompanied by its incessant ringings and clackings.

Joe saw the inspector, jumped to his feet with six trembling extension leads in his right hand. Sweat dripped from his nose, torrents of it and things weren't helped when he saluted with his left [wrong] hand whilst splurting out a saliva accompanied explanation; "It's no me! It's the atmospherics!"

It rendered the inspector speechless. A first!

Alas, that did it for Joe Scarborough. I saw him only once more. He called in at the police station to say goodbye and I watched as he heaved himself up the flight of stone stairs, suitcase in hand for one last time. He was off to another life in another place and I often think of him to this day, wondering what became of him.

But I'd seen failure. And failure for me meant the pit. Time to buck my ideas up!

THE MAD MONK

As it happened, my new found resolve coincided with the decision of Sergeant Keating to put me under the tuition of Aiden Fitzgerald or the Mad Monk to his contemporaries.

In a previous existence, back home in Southern Ireland, Aiden had been a monk. I kid you not. He'd arrived on the steps of the police headquarters in Wakefield one day with a, "I've cum ti' join yer." No exchange of letters, no sitting of exams, no checking of credentials or testimonials. Only – "I've cum ti' join yer."

And he stayed. Perhaps it was his cheeky, cheery, gap-toothed smile and a sense of humour second to none.

Good news! He kept me in the job.

Bad news! Shall we say he had some bad habits – if you'll excuse the pun!

Some examples to get you into the mind-set of 1960's policing:

AIDAN RULES OKAY!

Number one of Aiden's rules: You had to rule the streets, something ex-Constable Scarborough singularly failed to do. To rule the streets you had to get the local criminal underclass to respect you. The only way to do that was through fear – theirs, not yours. Yours had to be fought down in a very private battle.

Enter Aiden. I'd actually first met him in unfortunate circumstances late one evening. I was on foot patrol when I stumbled across our C.I.D. vehicle apparently abandoned in the middle of the road with its doors standing wide open.

Immediately, I was aware of a crowd of people in the yard at the side of a public house. From the noise it was obvious a fight was in progress. I waded through the crowd of bystanders only to find this large, ungainly man in civilian clothes punching one man he was holding against a wall whilst restraining another by using the simple expedient of standing on his throat.

I knew the big chap was one of ours, but nothing about him except he was engaged in aide to C.I.D. duties. I approach. "Would you like a hand, sir?" [Everyone was 'sir' until I knew them.]

He looked me up and down. "No thanks, son. I can manage."

That put me in a bit of a predicament. Not having any idea what to do next, after a few seconds I began to wander off. That didn't please the crowd. They began barracking, "Do your job!" "Coward!" "Stop them!" "Not old enough to shave!"

It certainly disintegrated any confidence I'd slowly begun to build up. Only I knew I couldn't explain to the mob that it was a policeman beating up the two men. I kept on walking, feeling rotten at my own inadequacies.

RAZOR MAN

Later, when Aiden was returned to uniform duties, he introduced me to a local nasty called Tommy Moore. He was a small, shifty man with thin features, a filthy mouth and could always be found on the periphery of any street or bar brawl. Not involved, you understand, just waiting his chance.

Because Tommy was a razor man! He liked nothing better than to sidle up behind a group otherwise involved and then slink away after a couple of quick slashes. It was easy to do, because that's the thing with razors or Stanley knives – you don't feel the damage they've done straight away.

"Tommy!" Aiden, the Mad Monk, shouted across the street.

Tommy glared back.

"You're in the book for obscene language."

"You ….." Tommy replied using plenty of words ending with 'ing.'

Unperturbed, Aiden removed his pocket note book and, after licking the tip of his police issue indelible pencil, began to write. "That's cost you a five pound fine already Tommy. I told you to stay out of my way. Now go away!"

With that, the odious creature shuffled off: A game which was played out over and over again.

But that was the thing – Tommy never bothered the Mad Monk. He always did as he was told – especially after Aiden picked him up one day, tucked him under one arm and walked him through the town.

MONTY

Later, it was my turn to put into practice the lessons Aiden had been imparting.

Maxwell Montgomery! Everyone in the town was a little fearful of him - and I include his mother in that. A young bloke, he'd been in trouble from early childhood. And now he was in his prime – large shoulders, muscles on his eyebrows - that sort of thing from hard work tarmacadaming the roads and from fighting in the travelling boxing booths which accompanied the gypsy fairs.

At pub kicking out time one night, Monty decided to stick a beer glass in someone's face. He'd left with his hangers-on before Aiden and I got there. So we began a search for him.

And there they were, not two hundred yards away, mooching about in the shadowy graveyard of an old and abandoned Wesleyan chapel.

"Okay!" says Aiden, as we make our approach. "You arrest him without turning this into the Gunfight at the O.K. Coral."

It was the first time I'd met Maxwell, although I'd heard of his reputation for violence, so it was with some relief, [not much to be honest,] when an idea sprung into my head. It must have been because of the stress of the situation as Monty's Indians were beginning to encircle the Mad Monk and me. One thing was for certain, unlike the films, no cavalry were likely to charge up and rescue us.

"Tell you what, Monty," I said with more conviction than I felt. "I'll fight you one to one. If I win, I lock you up. If you win, off you go."

Now, one of my granddads had been a bare-knuckle boxing champion at the pit where he worked, so I felt that maybe he was sitting on my shoulder. Stupid I know – I don't need to be told.

Both Monty and I were over six feet tall, but he was stronger than me by a whole lot. However, I had a lot more to lose. Prison held no fears for him but the waiting pit evened things up a bit.

I didn't dare look at Aiden's face as I handed him my uniform jacket and helmet.

Anyway, we set to in the middle of the circle of Monty's mates all of whom were cheering him on. I couldn't knock him down, but the drink had dulled him a bit so he couldn't put me down either. Eventually granddad intervened. Monty accidentally tripped backwards over one of the raised edger's surrounding a grave. Down he went. Not being one to look a gift horse in the mouth, I dropped my full weight of fifteen stones onto his chest and belly.

"Ugh!" The really weird sound bubbled out of him in a rush.

For good measure I thought I'd strangle him for a while.

He eventually got three years for glassing the bloke in the pub, but from our first meeting I never had one bit of trouble from him or his gang. He'd acknowledge me in the street, even when I was off duty -"All right, Mr Patterson" – and disappear.

Of course none of that could be reported to my supervisors at the time. However, I'd been well and truly 'blooded' – and the confidence it engendered undoubtedly saved my career.

DECISION TIME

It was approaching the make-your-mind-up-time for Sergeant Keating and Inspector Masterton. Would they recommend I be kept on after my two year probationary period?

I was on station duties one night and alone with only the coal fire, the A1 telephone and the draughts for company, when someone banged on the small, opaque window of the public counter. It was Tommy Moore, the razor man and he was drunk. From what I could understand he wanted to cut a copper's throat. Nothing personal – any copper would do.

Unbeknownst to me, Sergeant Keating and Inspector Masterton had been approaching the town hall when they saw Tommy staggering through the swing doors and disappearing down the stone steps. "We'll wait here, Sergeant," Masterton ordered. "See how the young 'un does."

Their wait was a brief one. I'd taken hold of Tommy by the collar and seat of his trousers, run him up the stairs and thrown him bodily out into the street. "And stay out," I said.

Any further conversation was prevented by the arrival of the two supervisory officers in the pool of light by the door. "Well done, Constable Patterson," said the inspector stepping over the prostrate figure. "You'll do for me."

That was it. I was IN.

TRIAL BY JURY?

The night shift continued to be my favourite shift of all. Much more interesting 'stuff' went on when the supervisors weren't around.

One such example involved a drunk in the cells. He was frequently locked up as he was one of those who became a fighter in drink. Unfortunately, it was his wife whom he used to beat. It was also the third time that week he'd been arrested for hitting her, so it was decided to teach him a lesson.

At 2 a.m. he was hauled out of his drunken stupor and frog-marched along the echoing corridor, up the stairs by the inspector's office and into the Magistrates' Courtroom. The place was ablaze with light making the prisoner squint to see the judge sitting high up above him on the Bench. A magistrates' clerk held aloft a large legal tome and a policeman proceeded to read the charge: He'd murdered his wife.

You could see the prisoner was trying very hard to make sense of this nightmare scenario; his brow was furrowed, his eyes darting here and there. But befuddled by drink, his brain was fighting a losing battle.

After a short trial involving a succession of witnesses, including a doctor in a white coat, he was found guilty and sentenced to life imprisonment. That did it. He broke down and cried and cried. He tried to plead between the sobs but was carried from the dock and back to the cells to start his life behind bars.

He cried so much I nearly felt sorry for him, but the sergeant's refreshment break was nearly over and the court officials and witnesses had beats to walk.

Next morning, he was let out. No doubt he thought he'd had an awful nightmare. I'd like to be able to report that he never offended again – only I don't know. I hope he didn't for his wife's sake.

NIGHT SHIFTS

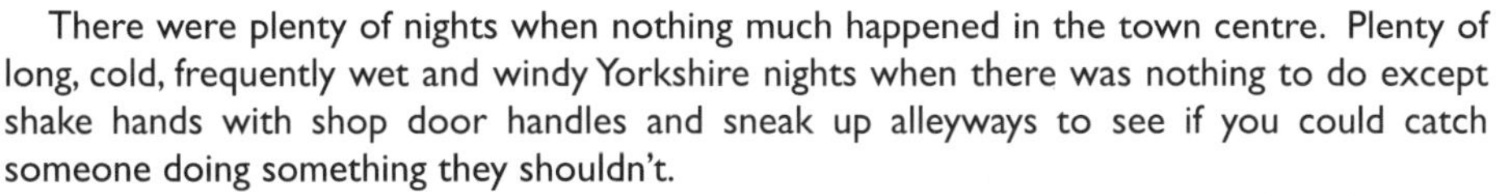

There were plenty of nights when nothing much happened in the town centre. Plenty of long, cold, frequently wet and windy Yorkshire nights when there was nothing to do except shake hands with shop door handles and sneak up alleyways to see if you could catch someone doing something they shouldn't.

Occasionally you did. A colleague once found someone breaking into a shirt shop. He decided to get help in the only way he could – by blowing his police whistle. And he blew and he blew, but no one came. A bit less blowing and a bit more running and who knows, he might have caught him.

But usually, the only thing you got behind the shops was a fright. The common police practice was to select a shop, usually one that had been broken into before [offenders often come back] then stand silently wrapped in your cape so as to become part of the total darkness. Your ears strain, you hardly dare breathe, you will someone to come.

After a while, you become aware of every tiny noise, a breath of wind, an animal scuttling by. But cats don't ever make a noise. The first you know of their presence is when they brush around your legs, or worse, when they jump over your shoulder from some low roof or other.

That's real fear, although one constable I know wouldn't agree. For him rats were worse than cats.

DON AND THE RAT

I met Don at a crossroads in town where our respective beats joined. A couple minutes chat to break the night up wouldn't hurt anyone, although such activity was totally illegal of course. Even being on the wrong side of the street could lead to punishment – but even Sergeant Keating couldn't be everywhere all the time. Well, that was the theory.

Anyway, it was three in the morning and bitterly cold, so both of us were wearing our heavy, woollen greatcoats. As we spoke, there were the sounds of a great commotion coming toward us: Totally alien sounds and at first, seemingly from an invisible source.

Then, within seconds, the biggest rat you've ever seen came into view. This guy was the king of all sewer rats and was being pursued by a cat, a mere six inches from its tail. The rat continually swivelled as it ran, clawing wildly at its pursuer. Not that the cat was being deterred.

The battle got ever closer, but fortunately was taking place on the other side of the street.

"Let's put our torches on," Don suggested. "The cat'll be able to see better."

So like a couple of idiots we did, catching the rat in two beams of light which would have graced any drama about Second World War bombers.

Without breaking stride, the rat turned at ninety degrees and ran straight at us, the cat immediately behind. The rat never deviated from the light beams. It came on at us – and fast.

Now, I hate rats as much as Don and was certainly quicker on the uptake than my friend. I switched my torch off.

He didn't.

The rat ran at his light, went up his leg, up his sleeve, onto his shoulder – the cat still following. The rat leapt for the pub wall behind us and somehow flattened itself into a hole that you couldn't get your car keys into.

Don's screams joined those of the rat and cat – only his went on and on as the cat settled down at the entrance to the hole, no doubt content at the prospect of a long wait.

But we were off, frightened in equal measure by the rat and the probable arrival of Sergeant Keating seeking to investigate the source of the noise in his town.

RAIN! The Constables' best friend?

On some of those quiet nights, I'd always try and snatch a couple of minutes outside the Art Shop before returning to the police station for the meal break or to go off duty. In the window was a framed picture of the ocean, blue as blue can be with a wonderful breaking wave about to reach out for a breathtaking beach.

It cost £4.19s.11d. – And I'd got five pounds in the bank.

Eventually, I couldn't restrain myself any longer. I bought it with the milkman's money and hid from him on Friday collection nights for the following fortnight.

The Art Shop was a good place to stop, not only because it was a place of dreams, but because it had a broken gutter in the alley down the side - an important factor in every good policeman's armoury.

Why?

Well, if it's raining, a policeman will always find a place to shelter. If you work at it, you'll get a cup of tea thrown in with the warmth. One of my colleagues had a string of 'fancy women' dotted around the town who, I suspect, supplied more than tea. Another knew a friendly publican whilst a third was friendly with the stoker in the coal-hole of the hospital.

For me, it was the fish and chip shop. Help with the washing up; make the old boy a cup of tea and the world's your oyster.

The old man was the famous Harry Ramsden.

Problem! If you've been warm and dry and it's been raining outside, how do you fool your sergeant?

Answer! – Stand under a broken down pipe.

But there can be problems. One constable thought he'd be clever and left his coat outside strategically positioned to catch the rain. He calculated that he could stay inside for an extra three minutes. The only thing was, when he turned up at the station he was immediately bawled out by his sergeant and accused of neglecting his duty. He strenuously denied the allegations of course, but went very quiet and sheepish when the sergeant told him to take his helmet off. It was as dry as a bone.

10 p.m. – 2 a.m. 10 a.m. – 2 p.m. shifts for a week.

WHISTLER

But sometimes luck was on your side. One constable – the Whistler, so called because when he spoke he expelled the air between a gap in his two top front teeth thereby causing his 'S's' to be accompanied by a whistling sound – had found his dry niche in the mortuary. It had a kettle and a gas fire to compensate for the smell of disinfectants. However, the place was an absolute no-go area. The hospital hierarchy would have gone ballistic and the Whistler sacked. But he reckoned it was worth the risk.

One long night, he thought he'd earned a half an hours respite from the cares of the world. It was 2.30 a.m. and not a soul was moving in the town. So why not! He settled down and nodded off only to wake with a start. He checked his watch immediately and panic set in. It was ten past four and he'd missed his four o'clock 'point' – the nearest thing to a hanging offence if anyone had been trying to contact him.

He dashed out into the night.

He was lucky. Only fifty yards from his lair he bumped into his no-nonsense sergeant – an old army drill instructor who hated skivers and who'd had his doubts and suspicions about the Whistler for some time.

"Where have you been?" he demanded. "You should have met me ten minutes ago."

One thing about the Whistler, he was a quick thinker. "Sorry about that sergeant, but I've been checking on a car that I'm not happy with."

If the constable thought it was going to be that easy, he was mistaken. "Show me!" Fighting down his rising panic, the Whistler led his sergeant around the corner only to find salvation in the form of a parked car tucked away in an open courtyard. The windows were steamed up.

"That's it, sergeant," said the relieved constable. He'd never seen the car before, but it would have to do.

But if he thought the sergeant would leave it at that, he was very much mistaken. The old sergeant still wasn't in favour of believing the Whistler, so walked to the car and tapped on the driver's window.

After a few seconds and a lot of movement inside the vehicle, a man opened his door a fraction and poked his head out. He looked annoyed whilst his female companion looked somewhat bashful.

"Has anyone spoken to you whilst you've been parked here this evening," asked the sergeant.

"Yes! Twice, already!" came the short, sharp reply. "And I can tell you I'm getting heartily sick of it."

Satisfied at last, the sergeant walked away; no doubt happy that Constable Whistler was on the job.

Whistler was undoubtedly pleased his colleagues had been a little more diligent in their duties that night than he'd been, but his worries weren't over.

His shift ended at 6 a.m. and off he went to bed. At nine he sat bolt upright, certain in the knowledge that he'd forgotten to turn the gas fire in the morgue off. Only there was nothing he could do about it – except worry instead of sleep.

But nothing was ever said.

A HELPING HAND?

I can't leave the night shift without telling you a very unhappy story.

11 p.m. There's a disturbance outside a pub and two constables race to the scene only to find an attempted robbery in progress. The offender sees the policemen running toward him, so he's off to the races leaving his victim on the ground.

One constable gives chase whilst the other checks the injured man and helps him to his feet. He's battered and shaken but the offender hadn't managed to steal anything. He tells the officer that he's fine and if he hurries he'll still be able to catch his bus – it's coming down the street now.

The constable is not so sure. He needs a statement in writing – at the very least get the man's particulars. But just at that moment the sounds of a nearby struggle reaches his ears. Obviously the chasing constable has caught the robber. No more thinking time. "Wait there!" he orders the victim, and rushes off to help his colleague.

The assaulted man is in a dilemma. Does he wait for the policeman to come back? Or go for the bus? He runs for the approaching bus and therefore away from the police officers.

Wrong choice!

Two huge detectives had just left the pub. [I'm a six-footer and was fifteen stones at the time. I was also the smallest bloke on the shift – so these guys were massive.] They see the policeman go to help his colleague – and the man he'd been holding by the arm only moments before, take off running in the opposite direction. He was running as though the Hounds of Hell were at his heels – and he was running straight towards them.

After eight pints of Guinness each, it was obvious. The man was escaping.

The victim-cum-witness had thoughts only of his bus and was totally oblivious as to what was going to happen.

The two detectives move aside to let the runner come between them, then at the last moment, came back together, shoulder to shoulder. Their hands never came out of their pockets, but they hit the lad so hard that all his money was knocked out of his pockets.

As the coins fell tinkling across the pavement, he joined them. He was flattened – didn't know if it was night or morning.

Anyway, the two bulky C.I.D. men were feeling pretty pleased with themselves. They take an arm each and drag the unfortunate young man back to the two uniform constables - only to find them looking disconsolate as they brush the dirt off their uniforms. The robber had fled.

The two detectives dropped their burden at the constables' feet. "Here's your prisoner, son," one of them said – and left.

"But…."

"No need for thanks," said one of the unhurried backs. "Glad to be of help."

So, the uniform constables were left with no prisoner and an unconscious witness. A good idea begins to form just as the man starts to come round.

"What happened?" he asks.

"You were mugged, son," said one of the officers. "You've just proved that lightning can strike twice."

"Come on! We'll give you a hand. Don't worry," says the other. So all three trotted to the police station where the officers cleaned the witness up and gave him a pot of tea whilst the offence of robbery was recorded and a written statement taken down. On the question of the description of his two assailants, the witness was a bit vague – but that was so much the better. At the end of it all, the constables dug into their pockets and gave him his bus fare home. The all-night service would be there soon.

The young victim couldn't thank the officers enough as they escorted him to the door. Handshakes all round. He'd write to the chief constable expressing his thanks. He'd write to the newspapers.

Just then, two imposing figures appeared at the top of the stone steps and ambled toward the C.I.D. office.

"You know," said the young man casually. "I could swear those robbers were a bit like those two."

"Nah!" said one of the uniformed constables. "They're detectives. Been out looking for the muggers, I'd bet."

"Ah well! Thanks for all your kindness."

It will come as no surprise to learn that the robbery remained undetected.

POLICEWOMEN

It was time to get married. Patsy and I were only just spared the indignity of having to obtain the Chief Constable's permission after he had checked on her suitability. The necessity of complying with those regulations, dating from 1900, had been changed but equal rights for women officers were still a long, long way in the future.

For instance, women police constables only worked between the hours of 8 a.m. and 10 p.m. and were confined to duties seen as best suited for them – no doubt by their male senior officers. The women basically got the jobs no one else wanted – statement taking, looking after children in the police station, answering the telephone, shoplifters. One job they did in their own right - and did well, was that of indecency. And for their efforts they were paid ninety per cent of a male colleague's wage. Hard to believe, but true.

Nearly as hard to believe concerned promotion. Promotion for women was confined to their own department. With only one woman superintendent looking after the interests of every female officer in the whole of the West Riding, quick promotion was a non-starter.

And it was firmly believed that the 'force' [who was responsible remained a mystery,] operated a hidden policy: The force would not become a marriage agency. Why spend money training a policewoman only for her to marry a policeman and leave?

The result of the 'policy' was that women constables were recruited only if they were unattractive. Nothing else could account for the formidable ladies of the Policewomen's Department.

I know things are very different now, but when equality came and the female officers took their places alongside their male colleagues working twenty four hour shift patterns, not everything went according to plan.

TANGO NINE-NINE

In the late sixties and early seventies, each officer carried a list of silent burglar alarms, each premises having been given a reference number to prevent any criminals listening in to police frequencies from getting to know which premises were protected. For example, if you received a call, "Attend alarm at Foxtrot Alpha two three," you'd get your written list out to see you should head for Boots the Chemist, or wherever.

It was the first week of nights for a policewoman sergeant fresh from her departmental duties. Instead of being behind a desk, she was out on patrol supervising her constables. For the first three nights, at about midnight, a call had been transmitted to all patrols: "Tango Nine-Nine!" It was always repeated twice more - for the hard of hearing.

And for each of those nights, the woman sergeant had stopped patrolling and examined her list for the alarm it referred to. Yet she never found it. And this worried her as it was obviously an important call if everyone was to attend. Something was obviously amiss, but she was too embarrassed to ask her male colleagues.

However, on the fourth night she could stand it no longer. When the Tango Nine-Nine call was received, she plucked up enough courage and radioed in. "I'm sorry, but you are going to have to tell me where this alarm is. It's not on my list."

"Sorry, serge!" came the reply. "Tango Nine-Nine is the call for tea. We always have a brew around midnight."

'YUK'

A policewoman joins the shift. She parades with her male colleagues fifteen minutes before the start time and waits quietly. One of the men is talking about the late arrival of 'Yuk'.

"Why do you call him Yuk?" she asks, more for something to say to break her nervous silence.

"Have you seen him yet?" asks a policeman.

"No!" she replies.

"Well, he'll be here in a minute."

They all wait patiently for the briefing to start and right on time, a rotund, round-shouldered, overweight police constable ambles in. His uniform jacket is covered in old food stains, his shoulders in dandruff; his boots in mud. But nothing could detract from his undoubted ugliness; a smallpox ravaged face topped off by long, thinning hair, tufts of which clumped around his ears. To make matters worse, he had combed the sparse, long hair right across the top of his bald pate in an effort to hide the hair loss.

"Do you fancy him then?" the constable asks the new policewoman.

She gives an involuntary and heart-felt reply. "Yuk!"

"There you are then!"

TAKE ONE CHILD

The 'Heartbeat' series on television is one of my firm favourites. I find the antics of the police in Yorkshire in the 1960's quite brilliant. And someone must have done their research very well – most of the time.

In one episode the Aidensfield Police are getting a right telling-off for the poor crime figures that month – the detection rate is down and the sergeant is not having any of it. The old cop, Alf Ventress, pulls open a desk drawer and says something along the lines, "No problem sergeant. I've a few in here that will help."

And we all 'had a few' tucked away.

The system worked like this. Take one child [preferably between the age of ten and twelve years,] [criminal responsibility comes into play,] who steals some sweets from the corner shop. [Preferably Smarties or something similar.] One child stealing sweets equals one larceny [now theft.]

However, if that child gives – say ten of his friends a sweet each, boasting how easy it was to get them – you now have one larceny plus ten handlers of stolen property. Eleven detected crimes.

No wonder we continually had a detection rate of over 60%.

The Home Office caught onto that one eventually and said one crime only would cover our little scenario, no matter what.

So a game of subterfuge began. Send off one crime report to headquarters, wait two weeks and send another.

Then they caught onto that ploy – eventually.

But they were defeated in the end. The statisticians had no answer to the conversations going on in police stations up and down the country. "How many larcenies did we have last year? A hundred you say. And we're busier than last year? Well, tell them we've 119 on the books – odd numbers give such a reassuring feel to things don't they."

It still makes me smile when politicians get on the news talking authoritatively about crime statistics.

GETTING MOBILE

One thing the researchers of 'Heartbeat' did get wrong was the first attempts of the police to enter the 'modern' world of cars. Mobility and response was in – walking and talking was out. Unless.....

The police mini vans of 'Heartbeat' are now wailing and flashing their way over the North Yorkshire Moors chasing villains. Blue lights and horns a-plenty! It may look good on the television, but in reality when the first mini vans and Ford Prefects arrived in the sub-division, you'd be a fool to put the blue light on, emergency or not. Quite simply, they drained the car battery immediately, so when you returned to the vehicle – nothing! Zilch! You're well and truly stuck.

Back to walking!

'NODDY'

But before the police cars, came the police motor bikes. Well, 49 cc Velocette-type things.

The first in the force was issued to an out-station constable called Billy Oldthwaite. It was handed over to him with a certain amount of pomp and ceremony. Senior officers paraded in their Sunday best and smiled benignly for the local press.

Only Billy hadn't been given any training. After all, it was a bit like a push bike which was a lot better on hills. Or so the senior ranks said.

So, Billy set off on his new acquisition. He was in full uniform – still wearing his pointed police issue helmet and, despite wobbling about all over the carriageway, he was immensely proud – fit to bust.

Second day of tottering and he's not getting much better on the moped when the Chief Constable in the back of his polished, chauffeur-driven Austin Westminster is driven passed. Billy, balancing the bike with his left hand, did an immaculate military-style eyes right, threw up a professional salute, wobbled – and hit the grass bank at the side of the road. Off he came, not that the chief stopped.

Next day a telex message is sent out from the chief constable to all divisions. It would be perfectly satisfactory for all officers riding motor cycles to merely acknowledge their senior officers by a nod of the head.

The 'Noddy' bike was born.

BEFORE 'MODERNIZATION'

The mini vans and the Noddy bikes were an attempt to get the police into the modern world. Or so it was thought. Certainly, prior to their arrival there was only one police car issued to each sub-division for patrol work. And that was an improvement on the days when the allocated vehicle was only pushed out of the garage to be polished – then pushed back in again. In this way the vehicle would remain immaculate for the annual visit of the dreaded, Home Office Inspector of Constabulary.

But back to the modern world of the mid-sixties: The one working vehicle was allocated to one nominated driver. In fact, you had to have completed seventeen years of service before you were even allowed to get into it at all. Let alone drive it!

Of course, the inevitable happened. My mentor, the Mad Monk, drew up alongside me one Saturday afternoon when the main street was crowded with shoppers.

"Get in," he invited, reaching across and pushing open the passenger door.

I was grateful for the chance to sit down and never suspected a thing.

"How long have you been in now?" he asked as we slowly moved back into the line of traffic.

"Nearly three years now."

"Then you should know better."

With that he grabbed my helmet and flung it as far as possible into the middle of the road. Cars braked. Pedestrians agog!

"Better go and get it," he suggested, smiling that gap-toothed smile of his.

THE CHASE

Imagine! It's three in the morning and the roads are deserted. Two police officers are out and about in the single patrol car. They're tired, wanting nothing more than their bed when a car pulls out in front of them, nearly side-swiping their vehicle.

The other car is full of young men and it takes off in the direction of Bradford.

Without a thought, the two officers give chase. It's obvious they've done something wrong. The 'what' can wait; catching them can't. The speeds of the cars go up – and up. Seventy miles an hour! Eighty! The police car makes ground on the flat, straight sections of road, but falls well behind at traffic lights. The other car is going through on red, the driver having a death wish - unlike the constables. The chase goes on. The radio has been used but police headquarters say there isn't another police car for twenty miles. The cops are on their own - but commendably they keep going. And going!

For sixteen minutes the high speed chase continues until at last the offending car is seen stopping at the side of the road. Men disembark and begin to run. The police car slows; the 'observer' in the front passenger seat opens his door. He'll get one of them at least. The policeman is out….

And ends in hospital!

Disembarking at 30 mph is not recommended.

RABBITS, PHEASANTS AND DOGS

As young officers in the 1960's faced with the new technology of 'panda' cars and personal radios, we had a lot to learn. On reflection, maybe the old timers had it right…..

With four cars now instead of one, men began to go missing from the beat, but to be brutally honest, none of the younger element cared one jot about that. For the first time we were warm and dry – at least for most of the time! The order to park the vehicle up and walk was simply ignored – we were enjoying ourselves far too much: Car races in the snow, chasing rabbits for the pot around graveyards at first light and let's not forget the pheasants.

One of our new breed of drivers was Terry Gregg. Now he was a legend – he could go around a roundabout on two wheels. Furthermore, he was only five feet seven and a half inches tall and so shouldn't have been in the job at all, five-eight being the minimum height requirement. And his eyes were so bad the only way he stood a chance of passing the sight test was to learn the wall chart parrot-fashion.

But he was an excellent scrum-half from the Welsh Valleys and the West Riding rugby team was in desperate need of a scrum half. So the rules were bent.

And once in the job, Terry got away with murder. He might have been small, but to make up for his lack of height he always wore hob-nailed boots and no one ever questioned why he was squinting all the time.

Maybe it was because he was a dab hand at catching rabbits and pheasants in the early hours. He'd drive at speed at the wildlife and with a flick of the wrist would hit them with the sump of the police car's engine. A nice little clip to be head so as not to spoil the meat!

He was the best.

Then disaster!

4 a.m. on a beautiful summer's morning and he had a brace of pheasants in his sights. Bump-bump! And there they were flapping about in the middle of the road. Quick as a flash, Terry was out of the car to wring their necks. Into the boot of the police Ford Anglia!

Cock-a-hoop, we return to the police station yard to unload them into the back of his own car. A quick look! No one around! Snatch open the Anglia's boot – and out came a jet-propelled pheasant. Straight into his face, its beak catching him in the corner of his eye!

Hospital!

He was lucky to retain his sight and it certainly put a damper on the early morning quests for free tucker.

No one ever believed his excuse - that the legendary black dog of police mythology was responsible. This dog repeatedly arrives from nowhere to cause unexplained accidents - then vanishes into thin air.

But good scrum-halves…..

THE RUNAWAY PIG

And Constable Terry Gregg's life was blighted by animals. Always was.

A pig in someone's garden and so off we go. It took three of us a good twenty minutes to corral it, but as we had no idea who'd be keeping one on the council estate which strung out along the main Wakefield – Bradford highway, Terry thought it would be for the best to put a rope on it and tie it to a lamp post. The owner would claim it eventually.

Well, he managed to get a lasso around its shoulders and tightened it. [This is no easy job, believe me.] However, as soon as the pig felt the rope, it decided against being strapped to a lamp post in the middle of a concrete desert and took off.

Terry held on for dear life. He had no intention of giving up his prize, but by the time the animal reached the down ramp onto the M1 motorway, it was going so fast sparks were flying up from Terry's hob-nails.

We were collapsed with laughter and unable to help. But Terry was a good lad – he held on for a good quarter of a mile before parting company with the porker.

Later, the message pad read, "No trace of pig."

BLOOD ON THE WALLS

But not even Terry could organize a venison feast.

A courting couple had run over a deer whilst leaving a deserted spot in the middle of our industrial sprawl. How the animal came to be there in the first place was a mystery in itself; but there it was, badly injured and putting the pair of illicit lovers in a quandary.

However, they did the right thing and carried it into the police station on a blood soaked, flattened cardboard box. They were reassured about the animal, that it was in good hands - and that their secret was safe. No one need ever know.

It was obvious to everyone who saw the poor thing that it would have to be destroyed, but whilst a decision was made on its future, it was dragged into the dungeon-like cell corridor. Question: An expensive veterinary surgeon and realms of paperwork – or venison for the whole shift?

So a macabre sight ensued. Two men dressed in white, plasticky-type traffic-duty coats and wellies slaughtered and jointed the deer by 5 a.m. The rest of the shift earned their meat package by cleaning up after them.

Unfortunately, in the cells that night was a young man who'd been arrested for breaking into a shop. He wouldn't admit the offence and so was being held for the C.I.D. to interview him the following morning.

Later, the young man appears before the Magistrates and pleads 'not guilty' – a surprise as he'd made and signed a written statement to a detective. In response to a Magistrate asking him about this damning fact, he said that the cells were a nightmare. There were strange noises outside his cell all night and come the morning he'd seen blood all over walls in the cell corridor. He was so fearful as to what might happen to him, he'd admitted the offence.

"Guilty!" [Well, what do you expect?] He was dealt with accordingly.

However, as usual, the local newspaper reporter was in court and as we'd got to know one another, he asked me about the allegations of blood and gore in the cells.

"Come and see for yourself!" I offered - and off we trod down the stairs to the subterranean, foul-smelling, Victorian dungeons.

The clean-up operation had not been a success. Whereas the floor was just about okay – the blood spatters up the wall had been totally missed. The Thick Blue Line had done it again.

THE GYPSY HORSE FAIR

Whereas all of us had been belittled by one animal or another – pigs, rats, cats, dogs, [especially police dogs,] my pet hate must be horses – specifically, gypsy horses.

Our sub-division included an annual horse fair, an event which attracted some wonderful characters from all over the country. They'd arrive with their vans and horses and tack and bring their vendettas with them.

Policing the fair was an education. Fist fights and knife fights usually arose out of the results of the trotting races or from a sale of a horse which had 'gone bad.' Many a time a horse or pony was sold, only to find that by the next morning someone had sliced through the tendons of its heel.

In the main, vengeance was administered on the quiet. But on one occasion all hell was let loose in front of my eyes.

A horse was being put through its paces by the owner who was running alongside it holding onto the bridle. Being drawn behind was a two-wheeled buggy, one shaft of which went down each flank of the animal and finishing just in front of its chest. At full pelt, this horse and cart hit another at right angles, one shaft spearing into the other horse's belly.

That kicked off a disturbance good and proper. Horse blood spurted everywhere, soon joined by human blood as the ruckus grew about me. The boxing booth emptied. It was as if the whole Gypsy Nation was on the move and taking sides.

And there I was – right in the middle.

What would you do?

I may only have a school leaving certificate, but I'm not entirely stupid. Taking on 'Monty' Montgomery was one thing, this was quite another. I slid out of the melee, content to let the Queen's Peace reassert itself in due course.

WINKY

Kenny Heron was a gypsy man who had a glass eye, so it will come as no surprise to learn his nickname was 'Winky.' And if the eye was ever knocked out of its socket in a fight – a frequent occurrence as he did enjoy a good scrap – he'd breathe heavily on it, polish it on his jumper and push it back in.

And fight! It was guaranteed if you ever called him 'Winky' to his face. That riled him to immediate violence and depending on how much he'd had to drink, he could be a handful.

It was a bank holiday weekend and Winky Heron had certainly enjoyed himself. He'd been locked up twice already that day – the holiday Monday – for assaulting a police officer on each occasion. Only he was such a nuisance in the cells, he was usually given bail. [The confinement sent him crazy.]

So there was I, clock-watching at the corner of Town End and eagerly anticipating the imminent approach of 10 p.m. - home time – when Winky appeared in front of me.

"Good evening, Mr. Heron," I said pleasantly, only to be greeted by a whole lot of words you wouldn't hear in church.

"I'm not going to lock you up, Kenny, so you're wasting your time." With that I began to walk off.

He grabbed my arm and put himself directly in front of me again, still cursing and swearing. Only this time he put his fists up.

"Mr. Heron! There is no way in a million years I am going to take you to the police station. I've got ten minutes of my shift left and I'm going home. Do you understand?"

More pugilistic antics!

"Go away, Kenny!"

Of course, he didn't go away but I could brazen the situation out for a couple more minutes.

I admit I never saw it coming. Somewhere from behind me and to my right a well-dressed man in a suit and carrying an umbrella appeared. Without breaking step, he reversed his brolly and hit Winky so hard across the head with the horn handle, that it felled the old gypsy. Spark out in the road!

"That'll teach him," said the concerned, pro-police citizen in a suit as he kept walking.

I was so astonished, I let him go. In fact, I might have walked off as well – only Winky's eye had popped out.

No one at the station was pleased to see him back, but the night sergeant accepted my apologies and locked him up for being drunk and disorderly.

After the usual paperwork I went home, leaving the night shift to let him go once he'd sobered up. But nothing runs smoothly in the Thick Blue Line. I learned later, that when the time arrived to bail him out, an inexperienced policeman had called him Winky as he'd handed back the glass eye with the prisoner's property.

Of course, the old gypsy went wild and threw the eye at the constable. Fortunately, it missed and twenty minutes later – the time it took three constables to find it again – Winky had calmed down sufficiently to be allowed home.

VEGETARIAN SUGAR!

The 1960's may have been the 'Swinging Sixties' for some, but for our West Yorkshire mill town, the decade was passing it by. Drugs still meant taking a couple of aspirin with a pint of beer – and we of the Thick Blue Line were not immune. We'd never seen a drug, let alone a 'druggy.'

Then one Saturday night a 'pop' group was coming to play in the town hall. Posters of long-haired individuals started going up all over the place.

It just so happened our shift was on night duty. The consensus was, 'If they're in a rock group and have got long hair, they'll have drugs. The fact that they came from London clinched it. None of this 'evidence' would ever get us a warrant, but undeterred we decided on a course of action.

Once the group had gone on stage, we pounced. Four of us – the whole shift – wandered into the deserted dressing room and started mooching about. After all, the law was quite obliging – if something is just there, you can use it in evidence.

And on open display - inside a guitar on top of a wardrobe behind some boxes, was a large packet. Whatever it was, was wrapped in greaseproof paper and sealed with sticky tape. We were just exposing the brown, squashy substance for closer scrutiny when the road manager came into the room.

"What's this?" I said in an accusing voice brandishing the parcel.

"Vegetarian sugar, man! Vegetarian sugar," came the reply.

"Oh! That's all right then," I answered, unsure what a vegetarian was.

It wasn't until years later that I realized we'd handed back at least a pound weight of cannabis resin.

Not my finest hour!

STRANGER THAN FICTION

Mind you, it wasn't just the police who managed to come across as somewhat dim on occasions.

There was once a persistent criminal who used to steal motor vehicles. Sometimes he just left them parked up when he fancied a different ride, sometimes he'd sell them. In fact, by the time he was twenty years old, he had over thirty convictions and was disqualified from driving until 2015. [i.e. nearly fifty years in the future.]

And he's due in the Magistrates' Court again.

I'm arriving to give evidence in another case when the young disqualified driver parks a car outside the entrance to the court and, bold as brass, walks in to answer his bail.

Of course, I follow. His case is put back so he can be processed yet again, so when he later appears before the Bench, he has additional charges to face.

In his defence, he apologizes to the court, before telling them that he now had a job in Middlesborough and wouldn't have been able to turn up if he hadn't stolen the car outside. And of course, he'd been forced to drive whilst disqualified, etc.

The Magistrates were none too pleased – with the police, [well, me.] "Unnecessary" was the word they used. The Bench saw no point in extending his period of disqualification but did fine him five pounds for each offence. A paltry sum which caused a little 'titter' to run around the court. [But I'll spare you that joke.] The reason for the small fine became immediately apparent – the magistrates had a whip round and paid the fines for him.

We were amazed - totally unaware there was a historical precedent.

Over a hundred years before, Annie Murphy from Tipperary had appeared before the magistrates charged with the theft of a shawl which she'd pawned. Basically, she'd been promised work in this country but on arrival there was no job. Without a family support system to help her, she was on the streets and starving. The magistrates were critical of the factory owner who'd promised work, dismissed the charge and gave Annie two shillings from the poor box.

A HARDENING OF THE BRAIN

But one should never underestimate a magistrate. They frequently get the better of the police.

One case involved the theft of ten tons of cement. From the outset of the investigation it was glaringly obvious to the investigating officer that the foreman of the works had been responsible.

Only he would not admit it.

So, the detective sergeant, [now deceased so I can tell this story,] did what all 'good' thief takers did. He helped the foreman out a bit by writing his statement for him. Unsurprisingly, the suspect refused to sign it. However, the law was quite obliging in that respect – no need for a signature providing the statement is endorsed by two officers saying it was kosher. In other words, the suspect admitted the offence but for some unknown reason had refused to sign it.

And that's what the C.I.D. officer did, endorsing it with the name of a detective constable assisting in the case.

The case eventually reaches court and the foreman of the cement works pleads 'not guilty.' The detective sergeant gives evidence, swearing on oath that the accused had made the admissions which he'd written down.

The accused is shouting, "Liar!" from the dock and is restrained.

Then the detective constable is called to support his sergeant. Only he'd known nothing of this particular case at all until earlier that morning. And now he's in a pickle. Did he stick with his sergeant and forget he was on holiday at Filey at the time, or…..?

The consequences of 'or' weren't worth considering. The detective was thinking on his feet as he was fast approaching the contentious part of his evidence, [i.e. after giving his name, rank and station.] He reaches a decision – and collapses in the witness box. Spark out!

As quick as a flash, the uniformed police inspector who was prosecuting the case was on his feet apologising to the magistrates: "The witness is a footballer your worships and yesterday he headed a heavy, leather ball. He must be suffering from concussion."

The defence solicitor is on his feet. "They are talking to the witness your worships. Stop them!" he cries.

All eyes follow his pointed finger to the witness box. The detective sergeant has the constable by the shirt collar and is murmuring sweet nothings in his ear whilst two uniformed constables huddled over them trying to give the C.I.D. men some privacy.

"Of course he's being spoken to," replied the Chairman of the Bench. "It's obvious they are asking him if he's all right."

The case concluded – and yes, the foreman got his just rewards.

After sentencing him, the chairman called the prosecuting inspector over to him. "I want no more heading of heavy balls in my court, Mr. Inspector. Do you understand?"

And everyone understood.

THE WAR HERO

These type of incidents were not one-off's. Obviously you can't support what went on in the name of justice – it's only that the game everyone played back then was different. It was a different society then and a different view of the police held sway.

I was at the Leeds Quarter Sessions to give evidence in a case of handling stolen property, [biscuits, not Smarties,] and was treated to a rare display.

The judge was a war hero and well known as being pro-police. Every officer heaved a sigh of relief when he was on the bench. The judge had lost an arm during the Second World War and always balanced several volumes of heavy law books along his stiff, false limb.

Anyway, this day he sat listening to a defendant trying to argue that the police had stitched him up when his notorious temper got the better of him. The judge leaned forward, moved his spectacles to the end of his nose and peered over the top of them at the unfortunate criminal in the dock. The stare was icy enough to bring the man's diatribe to a faltering halt.

"Are you calling MY officers liars? These men of high repute and good character who put themselves in the way of danger every day of their lives! And all for the good of society!" The voice was rising like a volcano until the judge, half rising from his seat, shouted, "You have the temerity to call them liars?"

The defence barrister was on his feet now. "I apologize profusely for my client, Your Honour. I'm sure he didn't mean offence….." Fortunately he stopped digging a hole for himself. One glare in the barrister's direction had been enough.

"Three months for the assault and three months for lying to this court. Take him down!"

THE DESTROYER

Christmas time was always a busy period for the police – and not all of it was work related.

A constable, Pete 'The Destroyer' McIntyre, knew someone who knew someone who fattened turkeys up for the festive tables. Now, Pete got his nickname as he was always on the look out for ways in which he could make a penny go a long way. He did this by cadging everything he could from sandwiches to cigarettes, or by looking for fool proof money making schemes. [Destroyer: - as in always on the look out for subs!]

Pete concocted a scheme. He'd take orders for fresh turkeys from all four shifts of officers working in the police station and for this bulk order he'd earn himself a free turkey.

But Pete bit off more than he could chew. The 23rd December was an unseasonably warm day when a dirty white van pulled into the police station yard. It was loaded with nearly fifty turkeys, all frozen and as it had arrived a day early, Pete was nowhere to be found.

A couple of officers stacked the birds, each in a separate cardboard box, in the garage whilst another worked the phones to try and contact the Destroyer and tell the men their Christmas dinner was ready for collection.

It was 8 p.m. before Constable McIntyre returned to the station, only to find nearly fifty officers waiting none too patiently for him.

Then the nightmare really began. It was pitch-dark and there were no electric lights in the old garage. That didn't deter Pete – he had a torch. Only the torchlight beam showed water running under the garage door. Worse still, the cardboard boxes containing the birds were collapsing in on one another so wet were they from the defrosting turkeys.

No worries! Constable McIntyre decided he would work quickly. "What size is yours, Tim?" he asks the first man in the queue.

"A ten pounder, please."

The Destroyer scrambled about amongst the mushy cardboard squinting carefully at bird after bird. It took him three minutes to find a ten pounder.

By the time he got to number four in line, the blokes were ready to lynch him. So, with panic threatening to set in, Pete hit on a new idea. He'd pick up the first bird he came to, guess at its weight, shout it authoritatively at the crowd and throw the bird into the yard. The blokes could sort themselves out.

It went well at first, the men being relieved to get their order and disappear. Some were due on nights soon, others already on duty and skiving. Coppers were shouting "Here!" and grabbing at the birds flying out of the dark interior of the garage.

Until we came to Dirky Wilson that is. Dirky - so laid back that it was a wonder he didn't fall over - he found it difficult to make a decision without a few 'mmh's' and a pull on his pipe.

"Fifteen pounder!" shouts Pete from the garage.

"Mmmh! That could be….." Dirky never got to finish his sentence. He never saw the flying, half frozen turkey coming at him out of the gloom. It caught him smack between the eyes – and down he went. Unconscious!

I don't know if Dirky came round in time for his lunch – or if he ever saw the funny side. But Pete's money making exercise from 'fresh' turkeys wasn't repeated.

However…..

THE KID'S CHRISTMAS PARTY

The Destroyer's next little earner came in the form of wet fish bought from the drivers who were delivering around the fish shops at night. That didn't prove at all successful when one night shift were so busy they forgot to collect the delivery.

The fish remained in its hiding place all day – on a low roof behind a shop in town. A complaint about the smell of rotting fish finished that particular enterprise, but Constable McIntyre thought he'd hit on a winner. – What could go wrong with bulk orders for fruit and veg?

This scheme involved using the police van to collect the orders from the market. Then Pete would use the scales in the police doctor's room to break the stuff down to suit the individual requirements.

Only, just before Christmas, Pete had collected a huge order. It filled the van. Even the passenger seat was stacked high. He was rubbing his hands with the thoughts of a good profit.

Then the inspector asked for a lift.

"The van's not very comfortable, sir," said Pete. "I'll get one of the panda cars to return to the station for you."

"No, no, constable. I'll be fine. Just run me to….."

"I've not got much petrol, sir." Pete interrupted in his panic. "You'd be so much better off….."

But one look from the formidable Inspector Masterton silenced him….. With a sinking feeling, he followed his senior officer to the loaded van.

"What's the meaning of this?" demanded the inspector, his face already turning red.

But the constable came up trumps under pressure. "It's for the kid's Christmas party, sir," he lied fluently.

"What party?"

That was a reasonable question as one hadn't been considered until two seconds before.

"We thought it would be good for community relations, sir. So a few of us thought we'd give it a go."

The inspector wasn't sure yet. "What good are cauliflowers to children at a party," he asked pointing at a box full.

"For the poorest parents, sir. Help them out a bit so they can have a proper Christmas dinner."

Masterton was gob-smacked. "Well done, constable. I'm impressed. I'll pass this on to the Chief Constable. Well I never! When is this party?"

"Next week, sir. Three days before Christmas. If that's okay with you, that is?"

"Certainly, my boy. I shall look forward to that."

It came as a bit of a shock to the rest of the cheap fruit and vegetable policemen in the station – but all set to and organized a party in double-quick time. And one of the must-have items for a party was a piano. Problem! The police station didn't have one. Answer! An appeal to the public in the local newspaper who took up the good cause with a vengeance.

Success! An elderly lady wanted to get rid of her old instrument and two officers were despatched in a police van to collect it. All went well at first, even though the piano was an old and very heavy one. But when the officers began loading it into the van, half way was as far as it would go no matter how hard they tried.

And the old lady didn't want it back. In fact when they suggested it, she smiled sweetly and shut the door. With nothing else for it, the two men roped the piano as tightly as they could and prayed all the way back to the police station that it didn't fall out. It was a long, slow drive.

They arrived safely and unloaded. Luckily for them the sergeant caught them at the top of the stone steps. "Don't bother lads. You've been that long we've had two others delivered here already."

"But…..!"

"Get rid!"

One of the constables was Tommy Little and like others of that surname, he was a rather large man. He'd always fancied learning to play but had never been able to afford a piano, so he grabbed at his chance. By now it was late, so after their midnight cup of tea, Tommy and his helper drove the police van with its commandeered cargo around to his home.

All was in darkness, Tommy's family having retired for the night. They tried the front door only to find the piano wouldn't fit through it. They tried the kitchen door with the same result. Finally, Tommy opened the old French windows which led onto his back garden and they were in. Much relieved, Tommy and his colleague pushed the piano into the room and left to finish their shift.

4 a.m. The phone rings in the police station. It was Mrs. Little. "Can you send someone quick?" She's upset and agitated. "We've been broken into. The French doors are wide open and there are muddy footprints all over the place."

"I'll get someone on the way now," replies the operator. "What have they taken?"

"Taken!" Mrs Little is nearly in tears now. "Taken! They've left a rubbishy old piano in the middle of my dining room floor."

P.S. The last I heard, the kid's Christmas party was celebrating its 20th anniversary.

THE NOT-QUITE DEAD

Yes! I used to like Christmas, if for no other reason than I was able to see an old policeman who lived in retirement on my beat. Every year we had to go and see the police pensioners to give them the Chief Constable's Christmas card, [to save the postage,] and to certify that they were still alive, [to save on fraud.] No nasty police widow was going to get away with drawing her deceased partner's pension. Not in Yorkshire anyway!

But the best thing was the tea and reminiscences of the ninety year old who must have retired when my father was still at junior school.

The retired constable had been stationed in the same dungeon-like police station below the town hall and in the room where we now interviewed witnesses, made a brew to accompany our 'parkin' or 'snap,' wrote up our reports, etc. he used to assist the police surgeon at post mortems.

For two 'bob' [ten pence now] he was expected to prepare the body – do little tasks like peel away the face, open the skull with a saw, open the torso and clean up afterwards. Oh! And hold the gas lamp whilst the doctor was busy. Gruesome! Yet the task fell to each and every officer who just happened to end up dealing with a sudden death.

I was just pleased it wasn't me.

But the story I enjoyed most, [he told the same ones over and over,] was the body in the park.

One Saturday afternoon, a woman had died in the small ornamental lake in the town's park. It was high summer and a bit of a drought had seen the water recede. He plodged out to the body becoming covered in thick mud up to his knees. It was obvious he could do nothing for her - the life-force had gone.

He waded back to the edge of the pond and then went and borrowed a ground sheet from a nearby bowling club. Back he goes through the mud once more and gently covers her up.

Out again, this time to find a telephone. By now he was caked in mud up to his waist. He phoned the undertakers, but everyone was out. Undeterred, he telephones the hospital and has a handyman bring a gurney down to the lake.

The man from the hospital duly arrives, but he had no intention of ending up looking like the Slime Monster waiting for him. He left the trolley in the care of the constable – and left.

So, the policeman had to manage on his own. He dragged the corpse to the edge of the water and, with a Herculean effort, managed to lift her out and onto the trolley. By now he was an inch thick in mud which covered him from head to toe. Only his helmet remained pristine.

By half past three on that busy Saturday afternoon, he was pushing the body of the drowning victim up the main shopping street of the town to the police station. Even though he had to stop from time to time to lift a dangling arm or leg back onto the gurney, no one gave him a second glance.

THE COCKER IN

I've introduced you to a few of the characters who inhabited my world during the 1960's. Some were good people, some not so good. But all were likeable in one way or another – all willing to play 'the game.' All but one – and he was a copper. Bert 'Cocker' Butters. He got his nickname because we were all convinced he was a peeping-Tom.

For years, people had complained of a 'peeper' "in a top hat." But no one had ever been caught.

And Cocker would go to any lengths to see into ladies bedrooms. He should have been locked up – but there it is. To me, he had no saving graces.

At that time, the sergeants patrolled the streets trying to catch out their officers. Being with another constable, not making your 'points' five minutes before and remaining five minutes after the appointed time, not being on your beat, smelling of alcohol, untidy hair, not wearing your whistle chain in the correct manner, not being wet when its raining, anything and everything was punishable. We lived in a constant state of, if not fear, then wariness.

Imagine then, a cold winter's night and Cocker had climbed a tree to try and get a view into a flat above a shop. A young policeman walks by below him, unaware of his colleague's presence until Bert whistles quietly, then nimbly drops down beside the young officer.

He convinces the youngster, who desperately wanted to be accepted into the fold, that he should make the effort, climb the tree and go have a look see. Foolishly, the constable does whilst Cocker keeps watch.

Within seconds the inevitable happens. "Sergeant's coming! Quick! Quick!"

The younger man had never done anything like this before and in his overwhelming panic, he makes a mess of things. His winter greatcoat, a thick woollen thing with an even thicker belt, caught on a spindly branch.

So, there was the policeman dangling from a tree at about ten feet above the ground.

Fortunately, Sergeant Thornton was not the brightest specimen in the force. [He'd tried to get a summons issued once for an offence of suicide. Think about it!] He had a florid face from too much whiskey, a fat belly from too much of everything – and was as blind as a bat. Not that he'd ever admit to it. He also refused to wear spectacles, so had to hold documents within an inch of his face to see anything at all.

Sergeant Thornton stopped and asked Cocker to hand over his pocket notebook for inspection. They chatted for a while as the sergeant slowly signed the constable's last entry as proof they were both doing their duty.

And all the time the young constable swung silently back and forth from the tree a few yards away.

Fair-do's to Cocker though. As they talked, he gradually edged the sergeant further and further away from the tree. And that was just as well, because the greatcoat belt gave way.

Down came the dangling constable with a clatter.

"What was that?" demanded Sergeant Thornton, swinging around. Blind he might be, but there was nothing wrong with his ears.

"Just a couple of Tom cats over by the tree, sergeant," Cocker replied. "Just Tom cats on patrol."

IS IT A DUCK? IS IT A ....?

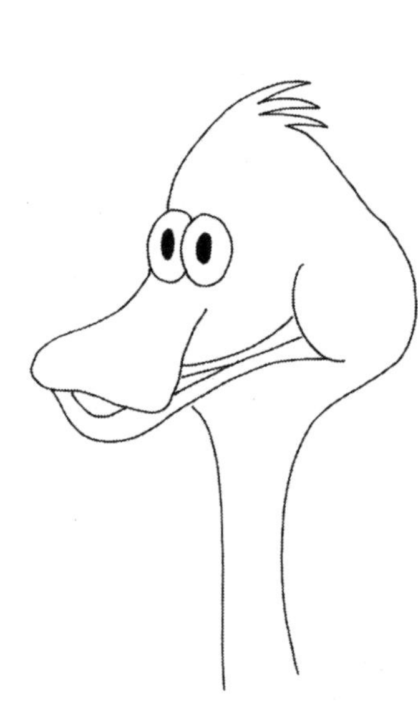

It was now 1969. My parents had moved from our Northumberland pit village to the West Midlands because of work. They settled in a rural village outside the county town and of course, we were anxious to see their new home – and take advantage of the free holiday on offer.

There were three of us at that time, our daughter joining us on our voyage through life with our son John due to arrive in short order. We couldn't believe the beauty of the place. There were countryside walks on your doorstep and an ancient town to die for. We fell in love with the place on the first day.

Day Two brought a stroll through the town's park beneath a parade of towering Lime trees. We're happy to amble along following the course of the river.

"Look at the size of that duck!" I cried. I couldn't contain myself. The bird was huge, brilliant white and skimmed the surface of the mighty river with a majesty which could only be admired.

Of course it wasn't a duck. It was a swan – the first one I'd ever seen in flight. You didn't get many birds of any description on the poisonous Tyne, [as it was then,] or on the polluted canals of the Riding.

Then realization hit home. I could get the same money serving in a rural police force in the West Midlands as I could amongst the muck of a mill town. Within twelve months we'd moved. The best decision we could have made, not only for ourselves, but for the children's future.

LIFE IN THE MIDLANDS
1970-1981

The dream of a life policing rural England, initially threatened to turn into a nightmare. It was a different world with what appeared to be different rules – at least at first.

THE ROYAL VISIT

Shortly after my arrival, Princess Margaret was to visit our town. A whole operational order was given over to ensuring her safe and speedy passage. No amount of personnel was spared. Every road junction and traffic island was manned.

Her official car would be preceded by a motor cycle outrider who would give a two minute warning of her approach. Plenty of time to clear the traffic!

At least that was the plan.

My duty was to keep a traffic island clear. It shouldn't be hard – the main trunk road went left to right with only a minor road crossing it. Not many vehicles, so the new boy couldn't get it wrong – especially as I had the assistance of a traffic warden.

We hung about and chatted, then hung about some more, when all of a sudden the motorcycle outriders [plural] arrived together at about sixty miles per hour. And Princess Margaret's chauffer driven thing was right on their rear wheels.

Therein lay a small problem. They'd come along the main road from the direction of Wales – a direction which had limited visibility due to a small incline and a bend. And I'd just allowed a farm tractor pulling a cart load of pig manure onto the island.

The traffic warden froze. He did nothing.

The farmer kept on going.

The royal procession was being enveloped by smoke from their tyres.

I was praying. "Please let the farmer turn left, go straight on; go anywhere. But don't turn right!"

The traffic warden watched.

The farmer turned – right, of course and headed off along the main road.

And that piece of road is double-white lines all the way. The Princess didn't see the funny side. Instead of travelling at sixty, she was crawling along at five miles an hour and being treated to the smells of ye olde rural England. So incensed was she, that she got her old mum to drop a line. "Dear Chief Constable, We are not amused......"

The result: Six of us constables standing in front of the Divisional Chief Superintendent who was definitely not amused.

"Why did you let the dung cart go in front of a Princess?" he asked reasonably in a shout to match his red face.

"It was passed me, sir, before the cavalcade arrived. The traffic warden should have stopped it."

"Traffic wardens are not subject to the discipline code. YOU are!"

All of a sudden, I longed for my job back in the mill towns of Yorkshire, places where royalty would never deign to visit.

LUXURY

There were two police stations gracing our county town. One was a non-descript, headquarters building where the chiefs hung out and transgressors of royal virtue were admonished. The other, the old borough police station dating from 1901, was sandwiched between two public houses on a quiet street just off the town centre.

And compared to my Yorkshire home, it was a place of luxury. No coal fires to light, a proper police club and cells that didn't look like medieval torture chambers. It even had windows. What joy!

Once outside on patrol, the town was a delight. You couldn't help but feel that you were walking through a history book. Old buildings, [certainly a lot older than the 19th century mills I was used to,] ginnels and letches to sneak through and wondrous things – like being able to walk around the town for eight hours and never see a piece of litter or a mound of doggy do-do.

But I soon learned that I spoke a different language to the local populace. Our Northern ginnels and letches were transformed into shuts and passages.

However, a difference in language can prove to be a boon on occasions.

THE VIKINGS

It was ten past ten at night when I left the police station on foot patrol. I cut through an ancient and dark passageway – and walked straight into trouble. Outside the Music Hall in the town square was a really noisy crowd of young men who were looking for some sport.

And I was going to be 'it'.

The ring leader was a large fellow. Give him an axe and a hat with a couple of horns on it and he'd be straight off the Viking boats.

I knew I was in trouble right from the start. Reason 1: He was likely to bite my head off and spit the bits out. Reason 2: His twenty mates were all bigger than me.

The leader sauntered over and looked down at me. "We're Welsh and proud of it," he roared. "Can you speak Welsh?"

'Don't say no if you know what's good for you,' a little voice was saying inside my head, so I resorted to broad Geordie. "Me la'? A' canna' even tark English, man. Not where a' cum frae."

I may have said more – but to my Welsh friends it was all unintelligible gibberish. After a few, long seconds the Viking began to laugh.

"He's all right, this one," he boomed. "Leave him alone. Goodnight officer."

I thought I'd push my luck. They wouldn't understand and it would make me feel better. "Aye, g'neet! Gan on awe yill miss yer bus haem. Yill ha' a lang wark thin."

But that was the thing in our little market town – at least during my early service there. The last bus went at about 10.30 p.m. and unlike our Yorkshire mill town, if the night duty constables didn't have an arrest by then, you were in for a long night. I've even known a man on a pedal cycle to be stopped three times whilst riding through the town centre at night. Each time he crossed a beat boundary, the assigned constable to that beat would flag him down, ask where he was going and check his identity.

DOG MUCK

So quiet was the town, that on many an occasion we had to make our own amusement.

Constable Jeremy Griffiths was a nice man. In fact, he was so nice he should have been a vicar, not a policeman. He was the most diligent of us by far and would never tell a lie. In his seven years of service, the most he'd ever dealt with was a herd of cows straying along a main road. Still, it takes all sorts and he was content with his lot.

One night, about 1 a.m., he came into the clubroom at the back of the police station for his forty five minutes of grub time. It wasn't long before the sergeant, Thomas Clive, was sniffing the air around the room.

"Which dirty b….. has brought dog muck in here on his boots?"

A short inspection by all those present and, "It's me I'm afraid, sergeant," says Jeremy in his low, monotone voice.

"You've got it everywhere. I've followed the trail from the back door. Get a brush and swill it away."

"Yes, sergeant." He looked at the ground, crestfallen.

"Then take the brush and sweep the street all the way back to your beat boundary. That'll teach you."

And he did, poor bloke. – And it was half a mile walk to his allotted beat patrol.

GARY COOPER'S VISITATION

Jeremy might have been slow, but on occasions my stupidity takes some beating. Take Gary Cooper for example.

This particular Gary wasn't a film star. In fact, he was nothing more than a nuisance criminal whose mouth got him into more trouble than enough.

I check the clock on the market hall. 10 p.m. Just another hour and I could go home. Time for one more quick walk around the block. However, before I'd walked twenty yards, Gary Cooper came hurtling around the corner.

"Thank God I've found you," he says between taking deep breaths and looking over his shoulder. "Lock me up for the night will you."

"No!"

"Please! There's a gang of Brummie villains in town looking to do my legs."

"Why?"

"A misunderstanding, constable. That's all. But they're here all right and not going home until they do me. Lock me up!"

"No chance!"

"Please!" he pleaded.

"Look! The only way I'll lock you up is if you go and break the shop windows of the market hall."

Five minutes later and I could hear a strange sound coming from the direction of the market. It was an irregular thump-thump, and sufficiently unusual to cause me to about-turn and investigate.

You guessed it! It was Gary Cooper. He was swinging his canvas knapsack and striking it with all his force against the huge plate glass window of a small supermarket. The glass would shudder and shake, but it hadn't broken yet. He managed two more swipes before I got to him.

"Pack it in, officer," he said, trying to shake me off and grab his bag back. "I've not broken it yet like you told me to."

"And you're not going to. If this window breaks, the shards could cut you in two."

"Lock me up then."

But I had a better idea. "Don't worry. I'll make sure the Brummies won't find you in a hurry.

"Great! A nice police cell will do fine."

I summoned a police car and my 'prisoner' joyfully climbed into the back seat. His consternation grew as the town centre fell behind us. We deposited him somewhere near Wales, wishing him a good and safe night.

From his colourful language, I gathered I was less popular than the Brummie Gangsters.

SHADOW BOXING

Yet, we had some rare nights. Nights when the Thick Blue Line stood steady in the face of danger and earned their corn. Only now, these nights in the Midlands were the exception rather than the rule as it was in Yorkshire.

The town boasted a professional boxer as one of its citizens - a young man who had the world at his feet, if he did but know it. He was rumoured to be a contender – a world middleweight champion in waiting.

Unfortunately, he liked his drink a little too much and frequently ended up in gutter fights. And one night our boxer did want to fight all-comers.

Being the new boy, I had no idea who he was, nor had I heard of his reputation. And my new colleagues were happy enough for me to put my best foot forward.

Never one to back down, I approached the Contender. "Now then, why don't you….."

He took a swing at me and missed by a country mile. Then again – closer, just enough to feel the rush of air as his fist went passed. Third time, he hit out so wildly that he fell over dead drunk at my feet.

The rest was easy. An embarrassing arrest, but at least I'd earned my spurs. The guys could trust me. But the story grew and grew – and before I knew it I had a new nickname – 'Floyd.' No doubt after the former World Heavyweight Boxing Champion with whom I shared a surname and little else.

But the boxer was a nice guy. Later, when we were bailing him out at five in the morning, I asked him why he drunk so much.

He replied, "I like it when I'm drinking it. But when it's gone, it don't agree with me at all."

THE ROCKET

I liked the name Floyd. I thought it was much better than Rocket.

Jimmy Connell gained his nickname in an unfortunate fashion. He was a 'panda' car driver and on this particular day he was allocated to the northern end of town - the busiest part. Anyone assigned to that area was in for a hard days work.

A '999' call to the police station. An accident involving a car and a lorry had occurred at an exceptionally busy road junction governed by traffic lights.

The communications room staff reach for the radio. "Alpha three! Where are you?"

"Alpha three to control," Jimmy responds immediately. "Drayton Road near the traffic lights."

"Excellent Alpha three. Attend a road traffic accident at those lights."

Fifteen minutes later and nothing has been heard from Jimmy.

So - "Alpha three! Situation report please."

"Give me a chance, control. I'm not there yet."

No one ever knew where Jimmy had been, but taking over fifteen minutes to reach some traffic lights twenty yards away – in a car – earned him his nickname. The Rocket was born.

THE POLICEMAN JOCKEY

Nicknames were common. Some, like Rocket, originated from a tale. Some were fairly evident, like 'Lugsy' for someone with big ears, but in our little market town, no name would ever compare with that of 'The Policeman Jockey.'

In November, 1880, there was to be a race meeting on the outskirts of town and six police officers on horseback were delegated to attend to keep order. All six constables and their steeds paraded in the town square in front of the public to be inspected by the Superintendent. Satisfied that all the bridles and saddles etc. were clean, that the men were well turned out and carried their long truncheons, they were sent off to the race meeting.

One of the constables, I'll call him Dick, took up his position near the starting gate in time for the first race of the day.

The favourite for the race was a nag to be ridden by the champion jockey. He'd over 246 wins under his belt already that season and was reckoned to be unbeatable.

The flag drops and they're off.

Unfortunately for our Dick, his horse decides to join in the fun – and takes off after the rest of the field. Dick dressed as he was in full uniform and wearing his heavy, winter greatcoat, police boots, long truncheon and helmet, should have slowed his horse down a bit. But the horse would have none of it. It's galloping for all its worth and the policeman has no choice but to hang on. He passes one horse after another. Into the final furlong and Dick is pulling hard on the reins, helmet dangling from its chin strap, coat billowing in the wind.

But it's no good. His horse is now neck and neck with the champion jockey's mount. The crowd are going wild. The professional jockey is looking worried. He should be cantering home not engaged in a dual with a – a horse with a policeman on the back of it shouting, "Whoa!"

The story has a sad end. The champion jockey won by a short head, no doubt heaving a sigh of relief. Of the fate of 'The Policeman Jockey' at the hands of his stickler superintendent, nothing is recorded.

THE AXE MAN

However, back to the twentieth century and ninety years later, I was with Constable Jimmy, 'The Rocket' Connell, when two incidents occurred.

The first involved our investigation into the theft of coal from a coal yard down by the railway station. And we had a suspect who'd been seen and identified by a witness. Well, sort of. It was more like, "I dunno! It could have been….."

Not enough to get a warrant, but we had to do something. You can't ignore information, can you?

We arrive at the man's house and knock on the front door. This scruffy old chap opens it, looks us up and down as if our uniforms were covered in dog do-do, then disappears inside leaving the door open. Not a word spoken.

Strange, but we follow him into his front room and tell him why we're there. "Can we have a look around?" I ask.

"No!"

"Well, I'll just take a look in the cellar," says Rocket in a friendly and chatty voice. "Won't be a mo!"

With that, the hard of hearing Rocket walks to the far corner of the room and opens the door to the cellar steps.

It was as if a light switch had been thrown. From total apathy, the old man was electrically charged and heading for the retreating back of the unsuspecting constable. And he had an axe in his hand.

From that point, everything happened in slow motion for me. I was running as if through an ocean of treacle shouting, "No-o-o-o!"

The whole thing must have only lasted for a second or two, but it felt like a lifetime.

I prised the axe out of his hand and told him, "Pack it in!"

I retired to the front door as Jimmy disappeared down the cellar steps. I couldn't help remembering a case where a policeman had suffered horrendous facial injuries in similar circumstances. Only we were searching illegally.

I'd already decided that a bit of give and take was in order here – I'd forget the axe, when I looked up to see the old chap heading for me this time. He had yet another axe in his hand, this time raised above his head.

There was only one thing for it. I started wielding 'my' axe at the same time as giving him a bit of reassurance. "You hit me with that and I'll hit you with this."

So we stood there, three paces apart in a Mexican stand-off until the Rocket re-emerged.

"Not a bit of coal in the place," he said. "Thank you for your cooperation, sir," he added as he walked passed the two raised axes and out of the door.

But that was Rocket all over.

THE SPRINTER

The second case with Rocket was just as 'hairy.'

Whereas I'd passed my police driving test in Yorkshire years before and had plenty of experience driving police vehicles up there, no one had ever asked whether I could drive when I arrived in the Midlands. And I was enjoying walking the town so much, I didn't bother telling them.

But sometimes you need a bit of something different. So, I asked Rocket if I could drive his panda for a while – unofficially like. Fine by him, so off we go.

Of course we get an urgent call, to a disturbance of some description outside a youth club. We attend with me still driving.

We weren't the first to arrive. In the yellow light cast by the street lamps, we could see policemen and youths milling about all over the place. One youth, in a black leather jacket, is running for all he's worth down the road and leaving an unfit policeman floundering in his wake.

"Get him!" the policeman shouts at us.

Engine roaring, we begin the chase – chasing this lad for some reason we've not been made privy to, but you have to trust your colleagues. It didn't take long to catch up with him.

We're close now - and he knows it. He turns right into an unlit passageway between two houses and I swing the car in behind him. Only none of us knew it was a dead end – not until the headlights of the police car shows this wall looming in front of us.

The youth stops and turns in one movement, correctly assessing that there is no way out. He slips as he turns, then starts to run again from a position which looks like he's starting the hundred metre sprint.

I'm braking. My foot is hard on the pedal, but the passageway between the houses is covered in gravel. And I'm sliding on it. On and on!

The youngster is nowhere near to his full height yet, but running, trying to get between the oncoming car and the wall.

Rocket, without any malicious intent, tries to stop the lad by opening his passenger side door. He's mortified to see the result of a metal door hitting someone in the face at 15 mph.

The kid goes down. And stays down! When we haul him to his feet, he's unrecognizable. A definite hospital case!

Problems loom. I'm going to get the blame for hitting the prisoner with the car door – or get into trouble for driving without permission.

I say a silent prayer, hoping the offence we were chasing him for was more serious than dropping litter.

It was.

HOWLING AT THE MOON

I've already said that you needed an arrest by half past ten at night, or your shift through until six the next morning was going to be a long one. You see, if you lock someone up, you may be able to stretch the paperwork out for hours. It's much preferable to facing a night of cold and rain.

You'll understand then, that when I found someone howling at the moon, he was worth a second look.

The night was freezing. Even the large, fast flowing river at the bottom of the steep hill had ice flows in it. And now, to add to my woes, it was trying to rain, the full moon slipping in and out from behind scudding clouds.

A drunk – if that's what he was – disturbing the Queen's Peace, might just do the trick.

I make my way to the Cenotaph at the entrance to the town's park. The human howling was joined by the howling of a large dog. That was my fault though. I'd tripped over its lead – a rope fully twenty five yards long, most of which was wrapped round and round the memorial.

"Oo-woo!" cries the man.

"Oo-woo!" mimics the dog.

"Blast!" I say to myself. Dealing with a prisoner's dog can be a pain – but a couple of hours in the warm beckoned.

By now, technology had caught up with the police. I have a personal radio. They are hand held and weigh a ton, but unlike yesteryear, I can now summon up some transport for my prisoner[s].

The transport arrives. Only it's travelling far too fast for the conditions. The drizzle is turning to sheet ice on the road surface. The driver of the police vehicle hits the brakes – and doesn't stop. He passes by the prisoner, the dog and me – all of us waiting at the kerb edge. I saw fear etched on the driver's face, his knuckles were white as he gripped the useless steering wheel.

"Oo-woo!" howl both drunk and dog as the police car comes to a stop twenty feet passed us. Unfortunately, it is embedded in the rear end of a parked car.

I'm just thinking the owner won't be any too happy next morning, when I hear another vehicle coming fast.

The premonition was overwhelming.

It was a police dog handler in his police van. The engine was screaming as he approached. He saw us standing at the park entrance, hit his brakes – and sat helplessly as the van began to waltz in circles along the road.

"Oo-woo!" howled the drunk as the dog van rammed into the back of the already immobilized police car.

Both drivers alight, slip on the ice rink that the road has become – and promptly fall over.

"Oo-woo!" cries the drunk.

"Oo-woo!" cries the dog.

"Oo-woo!" I join in, celebrating the fact that I'll be writing all night.

Yet, back at the station, it wasn't the dog which proved to be the nuisance. It curled up inside its kennel and went to sleep.

Not so his master. He banged on the cell door. He howled. He leant on the bell in his cell. He drove the other prisoners to distraction, so they joined in too. And all because he wanted his dog!

Eventually, the sergeant on duty cracked. The cacophony had given him a headache, so he re-united the prisoner with his dog – in the exercise yard. "Your dog's in there," the sergeant says, bundling the noisy drunk out into the freezing night air.

The sergeant's thinking was good – a couple of minutes under the icy stars would calm him down. Unfortunately, that night the shift became very busy indeed. More accidents! More arrests! Then a domestic dispute - and much more. The full array of nightshift woes arrived on the sergeant's shoulders.

It should come as no surprise to learn that the sergeant forgot all about the prisoner and his dog. After all, the howling had stopped.

Hours later, a full bus load of drunken young men returning from a distant football match, were arrested for smashing up their transport. They were all arrested on suspicion of causing the damage and driven to the police station. There were too many for the cells, so the sergeant ordered that they all be put into the exercise yard until someone admitted to the offence.

It was just as well the exercise yard was needed before morning. The howling prisoner was found frost rimmed and as near to hypothermia as you can get without your fingers and toes falling off.

His charge sheet was altered from the offence being one of drunk and disorderly to that of a Breach of the Peace under the Justices' of the Peace Act, 1361. That meant he didn't have to appear in court, but could be released without charge. Something which seemed like a good idea to everyone involved.

Ps The howling dog was quite happy in the yard overnight. He was in the kennel first and stayed there.

LOVE-HANDLES ARE GOOD

We never seemed to see a police dog in Yorkshire from one years end until the next. Not so in the Midlands during the 1970's where the police dog handlers demonstrated their love for their animals time and time again.

I think the handlers were the only ones who saw their dogs with affection. For me, they were dreadful mutts! All their training and they still couldn't distinguish the good guys in uniform from the bad guys.

Or maybe they can. Maybe they've just got their own sense of humour.

I was on duty at the town's annual show one year. You know the sort of thing – flowers, floats and fun. But trouble duly broke out after the pubs closed their doors following the lunch time session. One drunk tried to get to join the festivities without paying, before cutting up rough when he was denied entry.

By the time I got there, a tiny policewoman had managed to put a handcuff on one of her prisoner's wrists – then foolishly snapped the other end to one of her own. And he was a big, strong young man who thought it was great fun to swing this tiny girl about, her feet only occasionally touching the ground.

But help was on hand. A police dog handler was also involved before I arrived. With one hand he held onto one of the drunks arms, whilst at the same time he tried to keep his Alsatian out of the fray.

The dog was doing its bit, barking and snapping and frothing at the mouth. It was having a great time. But its handler had no intention of letting it bite the prisoner – too much paperwork.

I arrive breathless and sweating. It had been a long run on a hot day. I didn't have time to say, "Good afternoon," before the brute sank its fangs into my love-handles. I was lucky I was overweight. The fat on my hips just about choked it. Had I been slim, taken the doctor's advice, it would have disembowelled me.

To rub salt in the wound, so to speak, when we eventually arrived at the police station, everyone begins to fuss around the drunk – then the dog. They pat the dog's head, sit the prisoner down, phone for a doctor and begin to remove blood from his face and hands.

Only it's my blood!

ALL AT SEA ON A SNOWY NIGHT

Yes! I firmly believe that police dogs are fully paid up members of The Thick Blue Line.

It's a January night. It had been snowing and the ground had a good two inch covering of the white stuff. The storm clouds had passed, leaving in their wake a full moon shining down over a virgin land.

A telephone call: "My house has been broken into."

We attend quickly, the duty dog handler tagging along. From the broken kitchen window at the back of the house, was a trail of footprints heading off across the garden and into the park beyond. Perfect conditions for the dog to track the offender – or so the handler said. I felt like telling him that any one of us could follow that track in the snow, but didn't. Instead, we all silently acquiesced to his request to stay behind the dog so as not to interfere with it - interposing our smells across the landscape was a definite no-no.

The Alsatian was duly put on a long lead before the handler uttered the immortal words: "Fetch!"

The dog cast about this way and that, but seemed unable to find the offender's footprints.

"Sorry about that," said the dog handler.

"No worries! We'll just walk along and follow the footprints."

And that's what we did. After a five minute walk, the procedure was repeated.

"Sorry about that," says the handler.

"No matter. We'll just carry on, shall we?"

Another five minutes and still the line of footprints snake out before us - the only track in the snow.

"He's only a young dog, you know," says the handler breaking the silence. "Shall I give him another go?"

By this time we were in sight of an old Volkswagen camper which was parked up in an overgrown orchard. The footprint trail led straight to its side door.

"Don't bother!"

"Please!" the dog handler wheedled. "He's supposed to be fully trained. Give him a chance."

So all the officers present stood around and enjoyed the entertainment on offer. The dog walked about in circles, nose to the ground, ears flat to its head and ignored the suspect vehicle. The canine looked totally miserable.

But not as miserable as its handler! He knew he'd be the butt of jokes for months to come.

TRAMPOLINING FOR DOGS

Now, I reckon the snow dog had a brother.

We're called to a party late one night. Things had gone wrong and one young man had been stabbed. The offender had been held onto by party-goers until the arrival of the constabulary. Once the authority figure had arrived, the offender was handed over into the custody of a hapless constable. The officer then watched on as the man broke free, ran down the garden path and vaulted the six foot high larch-lap fence at the end.

Fortunately, a dog handler was just arriving with his dog. He immediately let the dog loose shouting some unintelligible command at it.

That night was wicked. It was cold, the blowing gale driving icy rain into your face with a force which stung the skin. But murder had been attempted and the culprit was escaping.

That fact mattered not one jot to the dog. It ignored the retreating figure, preferring instead to wander the garden before stopping to water a forlorn looking rose bush.

The dog handler's wrath was immediate. He shouted at the creature which didn't like being called worthless. You could tell that as it sunk to its haunches and began whimpering. The handler's fury turned to embarrassment in front of his colleagues. It drove him on. With all the strength he could muster, he picked up his Alsatian and dumped it over the larch-lap fence.

That's no mean physical feat. These dogs are heavy.

It was as if the animal had been dropped onto a trampoline hidden on the other side, for within a split-second, it was back. It vaulted the boundary fence, ran through the garden, passed its handler without so much as a sideways glance, ignored our group of sarcastically applauding police and party-goers – and jumped into its cage in the back of the dog van.

We all went to look at the dog. It was cowering and whimpering. There was no doubt in my mind – the animal was a coward.

The handler said nothing; not a word. Instead, he drove off with a squeal of tyres and disappeared into the night leaving us to our own particular pleasures of freezing rain, a gale force wind and someone out there in the blackness armed with a knife.

I was left wondering just who the stupid ones were.

VIC

I can't leave the subject of police dogs without telling you about Vic. Vic! The king of police dogs! The leader of the pack! In the wild, this was the top wolf. It was so ferocious that all the handlers were frightened of it – all except for its owner, Alex Easter.

And each morning, Alex had to don a pair of wellies before entering Vic's cage knowing there was going to be a new round in the fight for supremacy between them. If the handler ever lost, he knew that his dog would have to be destroyed.

So, with his soft-toed wellies, Alex would ignore the snarls and bites and proceed to kick the wolf-creature into submission. Once that was done, the days work could begin. And Vic loved to work. He was the best dog we had, especially in public order situations. It was what he lived for.

The trouble arose when Alex went on holiday. None of the other handlers would go near Vic. He dominated the kennels. Feeding procedures had to be altered after the first day. The kennel staff would put all the dogs' meals out into their bowls - then let the animals out of their cages to eat in the yard. That might have worked – but only until Vic arrived. He chased and fought every other dog until they were cowed. Then he proceeded to eat every bit of food from every dish.

Police dogs!

STUTTERING ALONG

But dogs have their place in policing and occasionally, particularly during some hairy piece of public order, you'd pray they would arrive. Football matches! Or rather, the violence surrounding them is one such, all to frequent, an example.

This story involves a really nice Irish guy, a police dog handler called Brian. The only trouble was that Brian stuttered really b-b-b-b-badly. You'd will the words out of him.

Supporters of the visiting team are leaving the football ground. It's not been a good game for them – they lost – and are now seeking to reek some sort of revenge in the centre of town. Facing them is the thin blue line, resolved not to let them pass. And for once we did the job. Plenty of arrests for breach of the peace, fighting, assault and what have you. So many, that even nice guy b-Brian arrested one of the hooligans.

Court day arrives and Brian is called to give his evidence.

"And what happened next, officer?" asks the prosecutor.

"The accused c-c-continued to w-w-wave his arms about sh-sh-shouting and s-s-screaming."

"And what was he shouting officer?"

"Get that f-f-firkin dog away from me or I'll k-k-kick it."

"And what happened next officer?"

Without a stutter in sight, Brian replied, "He kicked me firkin dog, your worship."

CIRCLE THE WAGONS!

A night club opens in the centre of town. It's the very first and pretty soon it was obvious that the younger citizens were no longer going to be content to go home at 10.30 p.m. Now, they were still hanging around, worse for drink, at two thirty in the morning.

And one night the police are called to a huge fight in the street outside the club. The whole night shift attends – all four of us. Even with truncheons drawn, the crowd is running amok. Reinforcements are urgently requested from neighbouring divisions, but they are going to take at least an hour to arrive.

The police officers - now embroiled in the fighting, start grabbing prisoners and pushing them into the police Transit van. It doesn't take long until it's full of bloodied officers and struggling drunks. The side of the vehicle is being repeatedly banged, then rocked to and fro. A bottle crashes against the back door.

It's a great relief to the officers when the handcuffs are in place and the vehicle moves off.

"Are you okay, Charlie?" asks the sergeant.

"Not bad."

"You okay, Bob?" The sergeant is definitely worried about what's gone on and the state his men are in.

"No worries, sergeant," replies Bob putting his head back and gripping a bleeding nose.

"Mike?"

"Cut lip, that's all."

"Great!" says the sergeant leaning back with a sigh of relief. "That got a bit hairy for a minute."

Several seconds go by during which time Constable Bob notices something about the police van. It's going round in circles. "Serge!" he asks.

"Yes, Bob."

"If you are here…..And so is Charlie, Mike and me. Who's driving?"

All four officers turn toward the driver – a shaven headed youth tattooed with 'A.C.A.B' across the nape of his neck, [All Coppers Are B……s,] and wearing a ripped tee-shirt. He gives a whoop, jumps out of the driving seat and runs off leaving the van's steering wheel on full lock.

The vehicle continues to circle as Constable Bob leaps out of the back door and flies up the road in pursuit of Baldy.

By the time Bob gets his man and returns looking as pleased as punch with himself, the sergeant has the police van at a standstill.

"Just as a matter of interest, Bob. What have you arrested him for?" the sergeant asks matter-of-factly.

"Taking and driving away a motor vehicle, serge."

"Commendable! But how is the evidence going to look in open court with someone from the press sitting there. You know – that the accused drove off in a police vehicle which was full of prisoners and had four officers on board. No chance!"

Baldy was sent on his way.

STRONG IN THE ARM AND ………

Same night club – different night: Yet another disturbance, something which was becoming all too regular an occurrence. We arrive to find dozens of people milling about in the shadowy half-darkness. The only thing that was slightly unusual was the presence of an ambulance.

My heart sank when I saw who was standing inside the vehicle. From the rear doors, a man was lashing out with his feet at the crowd below him. Tony Armstrong! Strong in the arm and thick in the head: And a nasty piece of work.

He wasn't hurt – just at bay, like stag being besieged by a pack of hounds.

The injured person was a man lying in the middle of the road – and his twenty to thirty friends weren't happy with his assailant. They wanted his blood.

The ambulance driver was in a state. His duty lay outside the ambulance with the injured man, but he didn't want to leave an aggressive Armstrong alone. There was no telling what he'd commandeer given a free hand.

I made the decision for him – drive Tony Armstrong and me away from the crowd. He was reluctant at first - until I pointed out that if he didn't drive the thing, I would! He could stay behind if he wanted.

He had us at the hospital casualty department in record time whereupon Armstrong decided to throw himself to the floor and began a series of convulsions.

The nurses ran to help, angels that they were. But I'd seen Tony perform before and the further any female was from him, the better. "Leave him!" I shouted, then "Get back!" Fortunately, they obeyed.

Armstrong continued to writhe in agony for a while until I nudged him in the ribs with a toe cap. He was on his feet in a flash; fists raised and ready to fight.

Years later, he really was ill. This time he was locked in a cell and suffering from the 'D.T's' or 'Blue Devils' or whatever it is you call it when suffering from constant alcohol abuse.

Now, cell doors are extremely heavy and have that little flap in them for observation and security purposes. Yet, Tony Armstrong frightened me that day. He'd put his arm through the flap and was lifting the door up on its hinges. I'd never seen it done before or since, but incredible strength all the same.

Obviously something had to be done. Either he'd hurt himself or have the door off. So it was decided to send two officers into the cell, protecting themselves with a plastic shield each. The plan was that they'd push him against a wall whilst I'd follow closely. At the first opportunity, I'd pull his legs from under him. The shield men would hold him down until we could get the 'cuffs on him and a doctor to treat him. All Home Office approved stuff and therefore no problem.

But the Home Office tacticians hadn't heard of Harry Hislop.

Harry would never rise above the rank of constable, but he was still as keen as the day he'd joined. He was a good bloke to have around in a tight spot despite the superintendent describing him as a 'dinosaur.' Only Harry was on a day off.

Ah well! We gird our loins. The cell door swings open. The two officers with shields advance. The prisoner is screaming something about his brain being eaten alive.

Then Armstrong's screams are joined by others. "Aghhh!" A figure hurtles passed me into the cell, bulldozes the two constables out of the way – and jumps on top of the prisoner.

It's Harry.

Harry the Dinosaur and Tony the Blue Devil fall over in a mighty, screaming tussle. The two constables discard their protective shields and get stuck in to. Everyone is rolling about the cell floor exchanging punches and grappling with one another.

So much for expensive equipment and even more expensive training courses!

But that was Harry – my friend the Dinosaur.

TROUBLE WITH THE EYES

Whereas my sergeants 'Up North' certainly were hard men and frightened the life out of me, I found a much more laid-back approach to life after I'd moved to the Midlands. The sergeants here were real old-timers who had nothing to lose.

Meet Theo Smith. He'd sit in the general office of the police station, feet on the desk and read the day's runners and riders at whatever horse racing track was operating that day. The thing with Theo was that he'd only plop himself down and get comfortable just before the arrival of the superintendent each morning. Being such a punctilious man, everyone knew the senior officer would walk into the office at precisely 8.50 a.m.

One morning, Theo was sporting a pair of spectacles. He'd never been seen using them before, but maybe he was just getting old.

"Good morning, sergeant," said the superintendent as he breezed in. "New glasses, eh? Good man: Good man!

"Yes sir," replied the sergeant dropping his newspaper a little so as to look over the top of it. "But I dunno! I still can't read the small print that well."

With that Theo put his finger through the empty spectacle frames to rub his eyes vigorously.

With a look of exasperation, the superintendent left for his office without further ado.

Theo's humour also extended to unfortunate members of the public.

I was at the scene of a road traffic accident with him one very foggy winter's morning. The road was a busy one and the crossroads we were at was a well known black-spot even with good visibility. And there we were, trying to push damaged cars out of the way whilst dodging oncoming vehicles. It was a hazardous occupation, yet with a visibility of no more than five to ten yards, we dare not stop anyone in case they were shunted up the rear.

A little old lady pulls up at the crossroads and toots her horn. Theo goes across.

"Can you see me across the road officer?" she asks politely.

"Just a moment ma'am"

With that, the sergeant runs across the highway to be obliterated by the fog. He shouts back, "I can't see you from over here."

BUMPTIOUS BESFORD

Another old-timer with 'suspect' eyesight was Colin Besford. Every time the superintendent walked through the office smiling and dispensing his insincere greetings, Colin would turn to whoever was nearby and say in a loud voice, "Who is that?"

A scene repeated day in and day out.

On one occasion I thought Colin had taken things too far. The whole of the early turn and afternoon shifts were paraded at 1.45 p.m. for a spot of military style drill. The superintendent liked to be reminded of his youth, I guess, but after he'd finished watching us march about, he took the opportunity to lay down the law as to how he wanted his station run. No lateness: No slackness; but just as he got to the bit about no slovenliness, Sergeant Besford walked in [late] and crashed the door closed behind him.

He certainly drew the superintendent's attention. Not only was he late – but his uniform was filthy. [In fact he'd just returned from a call to a chip pan fire in someone's kitchen, but he didn't let on.]

"Do you have to dress like a tramp?" the superintendent snarled in his best look-down-your-nose, acid voice.

He wasn't pleased – I can tell these things.

Quick as a flash, old Colin made his excuse. "Sorry sir. Lost a cuff link somewhere and it took an age to find."

TOENAILS!

Third on my list of all-time favourite characters was Sergeant Tony O'Neil. A short guy from Liverpool and a natural comedian, he should have had a career on the stage. His nickname was 'Toenails.'

Most people thought it came from his shocking handwriting where his signature had once been misread as Toenails instead of T. O'Neil. Not the case! I knew the real story – a sad incident which involved a piece of cheese and onion flan which slipped from his plate onto the mess room floor. He retrieved his supper, only to find someone's large, cut toe nail in the middle of it. Holding the offending article between two fingers, he held it to the light. "Mmh!" he murmured, popping it into his mouth.

His sense of humour was legendary. He'd been known to sit a dead body on a pedal cycle in the mortuary before sending a young policeman to investigate 'suspicious activity' in there. He'd replace someone's sandwiches with others sporting a half inch thick, furry green mould. And anyone he saw clock-watching at the end of their shift, he'd slow down their dash for home by nailing their 'bait' or 'snap' tin [lunch box] to the table.

But the best story he told involved his time in Liverpool.

The Greek fishing fleet had moored in the Mersey and were lying four deep out into the river from the quayside. One night, Toenails was patrolling when he hears the sounds of carousing coming from one of the boats furthest out into the river. Not only was it an offence against the bye-laws to have such parties on board, but no watchman had been placed on the boats. Another transgression!

So Toenails heads out to the boat with the party, stepping from one bobbing deck to another. On arrival he's met by a Greek fisherman who can only speak broken English and grin.

"You are not allowed to party out on the river," he tries to explain. Incomprehension follows, so he starts to jig about in time with the music coming from below decks. "No party!"

"Party! Yes! You come!"

"No! No party! And you have to post a guard on the boats." Incomprehension follows, so Toenails stands to attention and marches up and down a bit. "Guard! Guard!"

"Eet's okay!" says the fisherman with the stupid grin.

"No! Not okay!"

"Come! Come! Party!"

Toenails followed the man below in the hope of finding an English speaker. What he finds are eighteen men and two women trying to Zorba dance whilst draining bottles of local beer.

"Party! Eet okay!" says the fisherman who led him below decks.

"How can you have a proper party with only two women?" questions the officer.

"Eet okay! Wun for Captain and wun for crew."

JACK THE HAT

Then there was Jack the Hat, named after his trademark trilby. Jack had been an inspector on the C.I.D. for most of his service, then, in the twilight of his career, he was unexpectedly promoted. Only it was to a uniform post. Not ideal – but it would improve his pension, so he agreed to take the job.

Only Jack's uniform no longer fit him. Instead of his 24 inch waist belonging to his previous life as a 2nd World War submariner, he was now a more rotund, beery 44 inches. But Jack didn't care. He had no intention of ever wearing a uniform again.

Then came the fateful day; Remembrance Sunday.

Jack was to lead the procession of police officers to the church, then to the Cenotaph. All the civic dignitaries were to be present and there was no way he could slide out of this particular duty. Only he'd never bothered to pick up his allocated uniform from headquarters stores.

A last minute search of the police station revealed a pair of trousers here, a cap there, a uniform jacket tucked away in the corner of a cupboard. He could squeeze into the items

– just – but try as he might, he couldn't find a pair of black shoes.

"Ah well!" he thought. "No matter! My brown ones will have to do. No one will notice."

Despite his bravado, the question of the brown shoes prayed on his mind all through the march to the church and the service. Later, as he emerges onto the steps of the church and pauses to take in a deep breath, an old man comes up to him, grasps him by the hand and starts to shake it vigorously. The old man is nearly in tears. "A brave man! A brave man!" he mutters before slowly walking away.

Jack was startled at first, but this quickly gave way to embarrassment. He knows he should be wearing black shoes, not brown and that he was foolish to think that with all these ex-servicemen on parade, they wouldn't notice. He was incorrectly dressed – okay – but to call him a brave man was a bit over the top.

The 11 o'clock silence is observed, after which an ex-Guardsman marches over to Jack. The man's back is ramrod straight despite the passing of the years and he throws up an immaculate salute.

"Just wanted to salute a brave man," says the Guardsman.

At that moment the local press sees a good photo opportunity: The immaculate, tall old man saluting the small rotund one whose cap doesn't quite sit straight. They snap away merrily.

It's all too much for Jack. His mind is in a whirl. The Chief Constable may see the picture, notice his shoes. In a panic he blurts out, "I know I shouldn't be wearing brown shoes, but it's all I've got."

The ex-Guardsman looks perplexed for a moment - then breaks out into a huge smile. "Not the shoes, sir – the military cross and bar. Only the very brave get those."

Jack's eyes follow those of the man down to his chest and for the first time notices that the jacket he'd borrowed from the station cupboard, is covered in serried lines of miniature medals. "Ha-hum," he waffles. "Err, thank you."

He couldn't get back to the police station quick enough.

PSYCHEDELIC MAN

But Robin McCloud must take the biscuit. Newly promoted to sergeant, he was as keen as keen. It was no surprise then that he was selected to lead a drugs raid.

Drugs were a growing menace, even in the 1970's, but the police response was slow. We still hadn't received any training.

Undeterred, the raid takes place. It's a success. Well, almost a complete success for everyone – except Robin. He'd been picking everything up, smelling it and squeezing it, before popping the items into evidence bags.

He had no idea what the spots were on the squares of blotting paper and it was all a mystery to him why he spent the next three days in hospital having psychedelic hallucinations.

It was only later that the effects of L.S.D. being absorbed through the skin became known.

THE DRUGS FACTORY

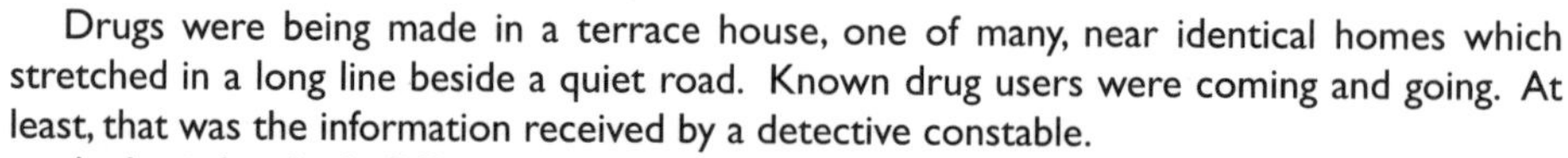

Drugs were being made in a terrace house, one of many, near identical homes which stretched in a long line beside a quiet road. Known drug users were coming and going. At least, that was the information received by a detective constable.

A plan is hatched. Officers will watch the house for twenty four hours a day, then, at the optimum time, we'd strike. Hopefully we'd take out the drugs factory and get some dealers at the same time.

Such dreams: Such flights of fancy.

After three days, the time comes. The detective, 'Stewy' Scott, who'd received the information in the first place, is watching the house. He's tired but keyed up. He's ready for action.

"Go! Go! Go!"

Officers swarm from the vans and head for the house. Stewy is there first. No one is going to steal his glory. He smashes a window in the front bay window of the house and gets one of the obliging uniform chaps to heave him up. He's in. Well, almost in.

As he fights with the full length net curtains which have entwined him, I walk to the front door, try the handle – and walk in. - All to the sound of breaking glass and much swearing from Stewy in the front room.

I'm confronted by a man in his fifties with his arms entwined about his frightened wife.

"Next door mate," he says in a loud voice to make himself heard above the crashing sounds from the next room. It sounded like the curtain rail had come down.

I must have looked stupid because he had to repeat himself. "The druggies! They're next door."

THE TROUBLE WITH V.W. MAN

The detective chief inspector wasn't a fan of drugs offences. He was one of the old school – could care less if people wanted to kill themselves. It was only much later, when druggies were found to be committing hundreds of burglaries or robberies to finance their habit, thereby making a mess of his crime figures that his attitude changed.

So when we were told a delivery of cannabis was expected at an address – the drugs for re-sale around the pubs and clubs – he allocated the man he could spare to deal with it. For 'could spare' read 'totally useless.'

'Totally useless' was Detective Constable 'Spitty' Williamson. Nearly at retirement age, he still ran about in a 1950's Volkswagen Beetle. His mentality was that he'd walk to work in the rain rather than let the car get wet. And that exemplifies the man – his attitude to police work was just about the same.

The detective chief inspector also liked his overtime payments and would return to his desk if anything was cracking off on the street. He'd never been known to get involved with anything 'out there' - but give him a chance to interview a man in the cells for stealing from his coin-fed gas or electric meter, there'd be no holding him. He'd do anything for money – just so long as he was in the warm.

The result of all this manipulation of overtime payments: instead of grabbing up the two men when they delivered the 'gear,' the decision was made to wait, observe and follow. Three little words 'Spitty' just about understood.

The property to which the drugs were to be delivered was a large, detached house situated at the side of a main road and about twenty yards from some traffic lights. Detective Constable Williamson took an unmarked police car and settled down with his flask and sandwiches just across the road from the house.

He didn't have to wait long. Two young men in an old car pulled up. They go into the house carrying a small parcel. Spitty radioes in.

Answer: "Wait! The detective chief inspector is returning to the office."

So, he waits and watches. After an hour, the two men leave and head for their car. No parcel. He radioes in.

"Follow!"

The youngsters gun the engine and are off with a squeal of tyres.

Spitty follows.

The two men go through the nearby traffic lights and turn right.

The detective sees the lights change to amber – and stops. He radioes in. "I've lost them."

It's a world record. He's lost a 'follow' in three seconds. But that's how it was.

THE DEAD AND THE DUMB

Incompetence also spread to dealing with the dearly departed. For the sake of decency, I'll refrain from the horror stories that any police officer, past or present, has to live with. But one or two are priceless.

Imagine a warm day by a tranquil river which meanders its way through a beautiful park being enjoyed by walkers and cyclists and flower lovers. God is in His heaven.

A report is received from a concerned citizen. "A body is lying on the banks of the river."

Constable 'Ticker' Purvis is sent to investigate. Ticker says he has a bad heart and can't do anything energetic or get worked up. [Just as an aside, I found out later that he had served behind Japanese lines in Burma and had walked two hundred miles on his own to reach safety. – So perhaps his heart was bad.]

Anyway, Ticker idles his way down to the river to find the body laid out just where he was told it would be. He can see it from ten yards away and that's close enough. He doesn't like dead bodies [Burma again] so gets a message back to the police station that the death is suspicious and C.I.D. should attend. A little bit of buck passing.

Constable Purvis hangs around well away from the body and after a fairly lengthy delay Detective Sergeant Charlie Whitelaw turns up. He'd lost the toss and is now by the side of the river. Only Charlie didn't like dead bodies either - especially drowning victims – so he gets no closer than the constable. The sergeant requests a doctor to attend in order to pronounce life extinct.

That's one little oddity I could never grasp. You could have a complete decapitation – but you needed a doctor to say 'don't bother with the mouth to mouth.'

A young stand-in police surgeon attends the scene.

By this time quite a crowd is gathering and old Ticker is puffing and panting, trying to keep them all back.

Only the police surgeon doesn't like dead bodies either. [Gospel true, I swear.] He stops twenty yards away, wrinkles his nose in disgust and pronounces life extinct.

"Over to you, sergeant," he says.

"Constable Purvis!" says the sergeant. "Go and search the deceased's pockets. Find out who he is. We'll have to inform the next-of-kin."

Grumbling beneath his breath, old Ticker heads over to the corpse, bends down and with his fingertips, starts to gently rifle through the clothing.

He's barely withdrawn the man's wallet when the 'corpse' jumps up shouting that he was being robbed, snatches back his wallet and runs off. It couldn't have done Ticker's ticker much good.

At the station some wag endorses the telephone message pad with the result: "Dead! But still breathing."

THE POST MORTEM

You see how the rank structure works: Doctor tells detective sergeant who tells the constable to do the dirty work. Here's another example.

A murder has been committed and the deceased has been found in the town's sewers. Someone had dropped him down there and replaced the manhole cover. Only it's been a hot summer and the victim has been down there for three weeks. I'll let you use your imagination - suffice to say that no one envied the officer who had to guard the body in the pathologist's lab all night.

Next day and it's time for the post mortem. The all-night constable is there to prove continuity of evidence. The detective sergeant is there, the detective inspector and even the detective superintendent from headquarters have put in an appearance. But they are all superfluous to the main event and stand in a line, against the far wall.

The pathologist begins. He opens the torso with his scalpel and immediately the innards begin to balloon through the incision. The smell of corruption is beyond comprehension. Now, the pathologist has a wicked sense of humour. He waits for a wind-filled intestine to get to the size of a soccer ball before wiggling his knife at the line of officers. "I suggest you leave," he says mischievously.

Of course the detective superintendent couldn't lose face and be the first to cut and run – so no one moved. Not even the young constable could be seen to be the first to break ranks. He wanted a career in the C.I.D. and so there was no way he could be seen to be anything less than the equal of his more senior colleagues. So he stayed.

They all stayed – whereas, in truth, they all wanted to go.

"No?" questioned the pathologist before turning away. It was too late now, for with one deft movement of the wrist he stuck the ever growing monstrosity with his scalpel – and ducked below the post mortem table.

The abdomen exploded. The vile contents went everywhere, covering every surface of the mortuary with a greasy, foul, mist.

The police officers were covered. The constable broke first. "Bugger this for a game of conkers," he muttered – and went. Two seconds later, the detective sergeant followed with his inspector hard on his heels. Another two seconds and it was the detective superintendent's turn, handkerchief held tightly to his mouth and nose.

And oh how they stunk. I know – I was that constable who wouldn't leave first.

THE LOST COCKNEY

Great thing: the rank structure.

By now I'd been promoted and moved to another police station where I had the pleasure of working with a great bunch of blokes. Only sometimes things didn't go according to plan.

One of my partners on the C.I.D. was Davy LaFrenchie. He was a revelation to work with having arrived from the Metropolitan Police, albeit under a bit of a cloud.

He settled in well – only it wasn't long before the Magistrates began remarking that since his arrival in the Midlands, it was incredible just how many local criminals had begun travelling to London. On being pressed to explain, all became clear. It would seem that in practically every case involving Mr LaFrenchie, his suspects were saying, "It's a fair cop, guv!" Or, "Cor blimey mate! Give 'us a break."

"Perhaps the officer might like to listen to what his prisoners are actually saying," a friendly magistrate advised me.

I was prosecuting another of Davy's cases. He'd done well to arrest a well known criminal for burglary, but the search of the house was undoubtedly illegal. The magistrates listened to the evidence and after a brief conversion with their clerk, the Chairman of the Bench spoke to me. "Mr Inspector!" he began.

I jumped to my feet. "Yes sir."

"What authority did your detective have for searching those premises?"

"Common Law, Your Worship," I replied with a lot more conviction than I was feeling.

"Very well!"

I sat down heaving a sigh of relief that I'd got away with a rather spurious assertion as to the Common Law.

The case drew to its conclusion. As the courtroom emptied and I was gathering up my papers, the Magistrates' Clerk appeared at my elbow. Harry Wood was smiling as he shook his head at me. "Common Law indeed."

He was well known to be pro-police and spent most of his time in the police club where he fed his wages into the one-arm bandit. So, I smiled back. "It's all I could think of on the spur of the moment," I admitted.

"I guessed as much – and so did the magistrates. Next time, think of something else."

A TALE OF TYRES, TWITCHY COPS AND A TELLY

Another character was Detective Sergeant Alfie Davis. His face was a mishmash of everything as if made out of left-overs: Nose too big, one ear a different size to the other, a lop-sided grin, false teeth that wobbled. Even his eyes didn't match - one blue, one brown.

But you'd underestimate him at your peril. He was a great thief-taker and I was always pleased to have him and his team on a job with me.

One such case involved stolen tyres. Nothing much in that you may say – only there were a lot of them: Tens of thousands of pounds worth. The information was good. The gear was in a lock-up garage behind some flats: Number 19: Third in on the left.

But there was no corroboration of the informant's story, a problem in itself. And there was no use in just locking the suspect up and hoping for a confession. He was a career criminal and would say nothing. In fact, he'd perfected his game. Not only was his home fortified and protected by Dobermans, but every time he went out [when not working] he made sure he was surrounded by a host of his children. That makes an arrest difficult – what do the police do with a van load of unruly kids?

No! In this case, I decided we needed some evidence to justify the hassle. Only without something tangible, the chances of a warrant, even for the garage, were non-existent.

Undeterred, four of us arrive at the garages which were set out on three sides of a square and overlooked by a block of flats. It's raining – lashing down – so we sit for a while in our misted up Ford because a man is delving inside the bonnet of a car on the track leading from the main road to the garage area.

We don't want witnesses around, so Mitch, one of the detective constables on board, hits on a plan. He emerges into the rain and ambles over to the would-be car mechanic. "I'm from the council, mate," he lies fluently. "I'm afraid we've had a lot of complaints about someone running a business from these garages."

"Hello!" The man emerges from the bonnet and is cheery enough. "I've only stopped to tighten the fan belt. Didn't want to do it on the side of the main road in this weather. I'll be off."

"Thank you for your cooperation," says Mitch.

Once the coast was clear, the rest of us emerged into the rain, one detective wielding a crow bar.

First problem: The nominated garage – number nineteen, third in on the left – is number twenty six.

Irrelevant! The lock is off the door in a flash. Empty!

We move to the next – then the next. No sign of any tyre, let alone a wagon load.

All of a sudden, the informant was being thought of as 'dodgy' and we're getting twitchy. And twitchiest of all was Alfie. His eyes rarely left the windows of the apartment block. Even now someone could be dialling '999'. The consequences – well, they weren't worth considering. We all knew what Alfie was thinking as he never stopped warning us about our impending arrest, our impending imprisonment for garage break-ins and his uncharitable thoughts about the nature of informants.

The fourth garage: Third in on the right and nowhere near number nineteen. Yet, there were the tyres stacked from floor to ceiling. Relief all round.

"Right! Let's go and get Johnny," I said, keen to press on and arrest the offender.

"I'm for the pub," declines Alfie. "Too much excitement for me in one day. Mitch can drive me back 'cos I'll be in no state after a few double scotches."

That left me, Benny Macklin and his crowbar. Not the ideal number to visit our suspect, Johnny at home. But we were young, keen and stupid.

Johnny Wilson was a well known criminal. He wouldn't get out of bed in the morning for less than five grand. And his end of terrace house was usually like a fortress. I'd never known this happen before – but the front gate was ajar when we arrived. His two vicious dogs could be heard snarling and squabbling to the rear of the house.

We knock quietly on the front door, hoping that the dogs wouldn't hear. A boy, no more than eight years old answers.

"Hello," I say giving him my best friendly smile, whilst half expecting a dog to launch itself onto my back.

"No!" He starts to close the door, but Benny gets a foot in first. He's more worried about the dogs than me.

“Is your mum in?” I continue.
“You’re cops!”
“Get your mother, there’s a good lad.” My smile is getting more forced by the second.
“Got a warrant?” says the kid.
“Yes!” Benny lied, not for the first time, and pushed his way in about three seconds before the dogs arrive and hurled themselves at the paintwork of the closing door. “Thanks for inviting us in,” said Benny.

The lad looked at us with disdain and walked off into the sitting room where he plonked himself down in front of the telly.
So, we were in the suspect’s house being ignored by the eight year old. We weren’t sure what to do next – although a retreat through the hungry dogs wasn’t something to relish. After a couple of long, silent minutes, a noise from the bedroom above.
Benny’s at the stairs in a flash, bounding up and leaving me trailing in his wake. Half way up and Johnny appears. He knows who we are and why we’re there. What’s more, he had no intention of engaging in polite conversation. You could tell that easily as he had a chamber pot in one hand and proceeded to throw the contents over Benny.
Not only is Benny’s upward momentum halted, but he screams, turns and bundles the pair of us back down the stairs.
Now what do we do?
I reckon that it’s unlikely he can refill the ‘guz-under’ straight away, so I convince Benny to give it another go.
“Be my guest,” he says, very subdued now. But the dogs outside haven’t lost interest in us yet or he’d have been away to the pub with the others.
I go up the stairs. Cautiously! Slowly! Benny is right behind me. He’s not even going to get a splash on him this time. I reach the top of the stairs, to the point where they take a right turn onto the landing and come to a sudden halt.
“Go on! Go on!” Benny’s encouraging me. He’s also pushing hard into my resisting back. He’s got his head down behind my shoulders for protection and so couldn’t see the gun Johnny was pointing in my direction.
It was a long, frozen few seconds before my brain kicked in and I realized it was probably an air gun. The pellet could put your eye out at this range, but was unlikely to prove fatal. [I love words like ‘probably’ or ‘unlikely’.]
So we went with a rush and took the gun off him. At first Johnny was excitable and full of himself. And why not: After all, he’d put the fear of God into one copper and made the other smell like a public toilet. But he wasn’t violent.
That changed at the foot of the stairs. I think it was the sight of his eight year old glued to the telly that sparked him off. A monumental struggle began. Mr Wilson had been known to pick up those large, concrete, roadside kerb-edgers and hurl them about like they were snowballs. So he was a handful.
But I mention this only because something happened which I’d never seen before or since. In the struggle, we careered into the television set toppling it onto its side still playing. And, all the child did was to move his head so that it rested on his shoulder and continued to watch, oblivious to the mayhem all about him.
The result! A deal! Johnny pleads guilty to handling stolen property, i.e. the tyres – and we forget the assault and gun pointing. A bit of give and take! As it was and should be for evermore.

THE NEW BROOM

I've just mentioned Detective Sergeant Alfie Davis deciding to go for a drink on duty, "To settle me nerves."

Drinking on duty wasn't unknown, albeit I suspect a little less prevalent than in the 19th century or early part of the 20th when publicans would leave a pint outside their premises for the patrolling night officers.

One story from way back then involved the arrival of a new Chief Constable who thought he'd adopt the 'new broom' approach before he – and his tactics - became known. In civilian clothes he sets off to test the metal of his men.

It's a hot summer's day and before long he finds a patrolling constable. He approaches the officer and asks him where he can get a pint of beer. The constable tells him that it was now outside the licensing hours, so that would not be possible. The man persists; "Surely YOU can get us a drink?"

So, the constable takes the stranger to the back door of a pub and knocks loudly. They are admitted without question and within a couple of minutes both men are standing at the bar sipping their pints. The stranger then asks the constable, "What would you say if your sergeant appeared now?"

"Why sir, I'd tell him I'm having a pint at the invitation of the new Chief Constable."

There's one candidate not to be included in The Thick Blue Line.

AND HERE'S ANOTHER

In the 1950's, there was a constable who was a 'drinker.' As he progressed through his service, the worse he became. If not quite an alcoholic, more often than not by midnight he was 'legless' – on duty or not.

His wife, Marion, was a large lady, the daughter of a farm labourer and had no intention of returning to the poverty which had so afflicted her family – a real prospect if her husband was dismissed from the service.

So Marion hit on an idea. It was quite simple really. After her husband had paraded for duty at 10 p.m. she'd walk the town until she found him and take him home. Then, donning his helmet and uniform coat, she'd walk his beat for the rest of his shift.

And they were never discovered.

A SURPLUS OF LETTUCE

One of the sub-divisional stations I worked at was no more than a pair of old semi-detached houses knocked into one. From there, a formidable uniform inspector held sway over a large, rural area.

Inspector Selwyn Powell is well into gardening and vegetable growing in particular. He has a large garden at home complete with greenhouses, cloches and sheds, as well as a well manicured allotment. Not satisfied with that, Selwyn also tended the gardens of the old cottages which are still behind the police station. Whereas he grows everything from potatoes to marrows at home and on the allotment, the police station gardens are reserved for his salad crops.

He is rightly proud of his achievements and the fact that he never had to buy so much as a single vegetable all year round.

But Selwyn wasn't a popular man. He was a good boss if you worked. But anyone found falling below his exacting standards was classed as a 'poor tool' and their life made miserable.

Not that these 'poor tools' took things lying down. Whilst the inspector slept, the night shift would diligently water his crops for him. There was no need for a toilet when there were perfectly good lettuce around.

And Selwyn never knew.

Being a generous man, he would offer free produce from his salad garden to anyone and everyone around the station, never cottoning on as to why his kind offers were always refused.

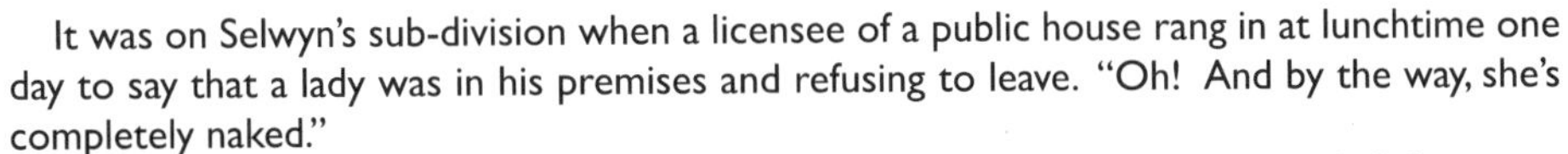

A LITTLE LIGHT RELIEF?

It was on Selwyn's sub-division when a licensee of a public house rang in at lunchtime one day to say that a lady was in his premises and refusing to leave. "Oh! And by the way, she's completely naked."

Police cars speed to the scene, but if the officers were expecting a little light relief, they were to be disappointed. If the lady in question was undoubtedly naked, she was also undoubtedly huge. Grotesquely large would be a better description and was uncooperative with it. She drew more attention to herself by continually shouting, "It's me burfday."

We didn't have enough constables to get her into a vehicle without her cooperation – and she would have none of it. Not that it really mattered because we didn't have a vehicle large enough to accommodate her anyway.

Time to compromise: We'd sing one chorus of 'Happy birthday,' if she'd go straight home. And that's what happened – even though she had a half mile walk through the town with its lunchtime shoppers.

JIMMY THE FROG

Compromise is a useful weapon for the police. For example, it was time to take a constable to task for failing to do his duty.

His name was Jimmy the Frog, so called because he'd make a frog look good. And he wore a toupee – not that he'd admit to it. But his wig was so bad a fit, that when he put his helmet on or took it off, he had to hold his hairpiece in place with his other hand. And Jimmy was as lazy as he was ugly. He would neither arrest anyone nor even report any offence whatsoever.

Hence my having to take him to task: This odious duty was brought about by an incident on the previous week of night duty.

A couple of constables had responded to a call about a drunk asleep in a shop doorway. Whilst trying to rouse him [unsuccessfully] they realized they had been presented with a chance to make the Frog do some work. They'd seen him walking in their direction and knew he'd be passing that very spot in a couple of minutes. So they pulled the drunk out of the doorway, spread him out all over the pavement and hid.

Sure enough, Jimmy appeared on cue, patrolling at a regulation two and a half miles an hour.

He walked toward the trap – only when he got to the drunk he didn't even break stride. He stepped over the unconscious form and kept walking.

Time for action: "Out there this afternoon and get me an offence," I said laying the law down to him. "I don't care what it is. Anything will do. Just do something."

Three hours later and I'm walking down the main street when the ungainly constable crosses the road, salutes and gives me a huge grin. "Sir," Jimmy began. "I've been up and down the High Street for hours and I've only found one offence."

"Good man," I reply. My pep talk had worked. I reckoned I must be good at this man management job. "What is it?"

"It's an expired tax disc on a car, sir."

"Well done, Jimmy. You see, you can do it if you keep your eyes peeled. Have you reported the owner?"

"No sir. I thought I'd speak with you first."

"And why is that?" I asked, hardly able to disguise my exasperation with him.

"Well….." he mused. "It's your car."

Compromise! That's the thing. I get a tax disc straight away.

GOOD INTENTIONS AND ALL THAT

And the good intentions of supervisory officers do have a nasty habit of going bad.

I was given charge of a shift and when the men paraded for night duty, I was appalled to see them turning up in shirt sleeve order, without truncheons or torches. So I waded in. "This won't do…!" "You will….!" etc. etc.

That very same night a silent burglar alarm was activated in a shop. I attended in the company of a sergeant who'd been on the shift for some time. And we arrived first. The door is half hanging off its hinges, so we burst in. There's definitely someone moving around toward the back – only we can't find the light switch.

And I don't have a torch.

And the sergeant doesn't have a torch.

Before I can stop him, he's on the radio. "Get someone down here quick. The burglars are still on the premises and the inspector doesn't have his torch."

Embarrassing! - But a bit of pay-back to the new boy.

THE BOYS IN BIG CARS

And I just used to love the stuff that office bound wallahs in headquarters used to come up with time and time again.

Do you think that anyone with half a brain would come up with this new title for traffic [or motorway] patrol cars: 'Fast Action Response Teams.'

We compromised and called them…..Well, you work it out.

THE SPEEDER

These FART cars were responsible for catching speeders using the radar guns. The two constables driving the patrol car attached to my shift were good lads. Both were keen, respectful and full of fun, so it came as no surprise when they said, "We'll get you for this," after one of my rare wins at snooker during the break time.

A couple of days later I'm in my own car – a car well known to my colleagues – and was heading for home. I wasn't concentrating too hard on my driving and I'd have to admit I was travelling at a couple of miles an hour above the 30 mph. speed limit. Then the nightmare! There was a uniform holding a speed gun – and it was homing in on me.

For some unfathomable reason, I immediately thought it was my colleagues, Jock and Geordie, pretending to get their own back for the snooker result. I opened my window, put my foot down and gave them a good two fingered salute as I accelerated passed.

The operator was so surprised at my reaction, he dropped the equipment.

He was surprised! I was surprised! I'd never seen those constables before in my life.

I didn't get a summons – the speed gun was in pieces, but I wouldn't recommend that course of action to anyone. I certainly spent an uncomfortable fourteen days, the time limit to receive a notice of intended prosecution, expecting one to drop through my letter box at any time.

Or maybe they didn't want me telling this little tale about 'traffic men':

STUCK UP AND STUPID

It's one of the busiest days of the year for the town. It's Carnival – a day when fifty thousand people descend on the place; a day when the traffic snarl-ups make the national news.

And that day of all days, a large articulated lorry decides to go under a not-so-big railway bridge. The inevitable happens. It's stuck fast and the traffic backs up immediately.

The two officers of our Fast Action Response Team get there in record time – all blue lights and sirens – then approach a fed-up lorry driver who's the butt of honking motorists.

"Are you stuck?" asks one of the constables.

"No officer! You see, I've got this bridge to deliver and I've lost the address."

STUCK 'UP THERE' AND STUPID

Toward the end of my service, specialization held sway. Gone were the days when a constable had to do everything from investigating a crime to making scale drawings of fatal accident scenes. Someone, somewhere would do it all for you: Experts in every imaginable field – including Working Committees scratching their heads as to why none of their super-duper, technical radios were working. They were great in the workshops, the technical 'bods' checked their 'mega what's-its' and 'hertz thingy's' and nothing was wrong. This was state of the art stuff they were providing to the police - yet nothing worked 'out there.' Then they asked a patrol sergeant to come and speak to them – just to get the common man's input, you understand. His approach appalled them. "Apply this test," said the officer. "Put the radio on top of a patrol car. Drive the car at fifty miles an hour, brake - so the radio scoots down the road, run over it: Then switch it on. If it works – buy it! That's about as much care as your equipment gets!"

But the new 'big thing' was Air Support, supplied either in the form of a police helicopter or a small fixed wing aircraft.

Nigel Avery was a failed Army helicopter pilot - he just couldn't seem to get the landings right. But that didn't stop him getting a job as an 'observer' in the new unit. There was a nice little opportunity here to create an empire. He could see promotion, his own fleet of helicopters.....

Not satisfied with this cushy number, his new job re-stimulated his desire to fly. So excited, so all embracing a passion did it become, that he ended up buying himself a little, one-engine job so he could do a bit of joy riding.

The trouble with Nigel was – well, I'll let you make your own mind up with this example.

He takes off with a friend to go for a day's racing at a nearby town. It couldn't be an easier trip as all he had to do was follow the main trunk road south for fifty miles. A major road is a necessary boon to your chances of survival when you haven't learned to navigate.

And why shouldn't he just follow the road down there. It was a lovely, clear day.

At least it was when he took off. Within minutes the cloud was thickening, being blown in on a freshening wind from the Welsh mountains. His sight of the road was coming and going. The cloud got thicker and thicker. But did Nigel turn back?

Nope! He decides it would be a good idea if he climbed above the cloud and into the sun. [I suspect that you and I would realize that you're not going to find the road up there – but not Nigel.] Up he went. And up! And up until eventually he broke out into the sun at ten thousand feet. He'd never been this high before and his sense of panic was transferring itself to his passenger who began to ask, "Are we going to die?"

Nigel could see nothing below except clouds and not being instrument trained, the dials and stuff on his dashboard didn't mean very much. "Do you know what these things are for?" he asks his passenger whilst pointing at the battery of gauges.

"We're gonna die!" the passenger began - then kept repeating it every few seconds.

So, a worried Nigel realizes that he'd done the wrong thing going up and decides to reverse the process. He dives down in search of the road again. However, after a few minutes in dense cloud, he was so disorientated that he didn't even know which way was up any more. In panic, he reverses direction again.

Being totally lost, there was only one thing for it. He knew how to use the radio. "Mayday! Mayday!"

"Hello, Bravo Alpha," came the disembodied voice of a cool customer somewhere in the ether.

"Mayday! Mayday!" shouts Nigel.

"We're gonna die," shouts the passenger.

"Bravo Alpha," the voice continues. "You are in Birmingham International Airport airspace. Get out! Now!" Not so cool any more.

"I don't know where I am. Can you tell me which way is out, please?"

"Oh! For God's sake! Just a minute!" After what must have seemed like a lifetime of loneliness, the controller at the airport is back on air again. "Bravo Alpha. Just circle there for a minute. I'll get someone to you."

"Will you ask them to hurry, please," says Nigel. "We've no fuel left."

"How much flying time have you got left?"

"I dunno. It's been on red for the last twenty minutes."

"We're gonna die!" shouts the passenger.

"Oh! For God's sake! Just a minute!"

The operator switches frequency. "Control to Helicopter 01. Please take this idiot in the plane at [coordinates given] and dump him over the North Sea will you. He's playing footsy with international jet liners here."

Within seconds, the rescue helicopter is hovering alongside Nigel's little plane. "Now that I've found you," says the helicopter pilot to Nigel, "I'll have to go down for a few seconds. We're so high my rotor blades are icing up."

"Don't go! Don't go!" pleads Nigel in a real panic now.

"We're gonna die," shouts the passenger.

"Oh for God's sake! Just wait a minute."

Off goes the helicopter, but good news. Not only does he come back, but the flight controllers at Birmingham International have given permission for Nigel to have one go at landing his plane.

The international planes are circling. All eyes are on Nigel.

"Follow me down, please," says the cool helicopter pilot.

This plan lasted about thirty seconds before Nigel overtook the rescue craft and breaks out of the cloud. Immediately our policeman pilot sees his predicament. He's at too tight an angle to land and he's way, way too fast.

But Nigel is passed caring. He doesn't fancy ditching in the North Sea, so he pulls hard back on the controls. He hits the runway so hard that he goes back up fifty feet. He hits again, bounces back to fifty feet. Then again! And again! It takes most of the runway that jet airliners use to stop his little plane.

Well done, Nigel! A fully paid up member of the Thick Blue Line!

NOT BAD FOR A SECONDARY SCHOOL KID!

It's 1981. I'm attending a Mess Night for members of the Junior Command Course at Bramshill – the 'Policeman's University.'

It's a warm, summer's night in rural Hampshire. We're on the elevated terrace of a very grand country house, sipping our G and T's and chatting whilst a herd of white deer grazed in the parkland below. Behind us, the terrace doors to the ballroom have been thrown open, the music from a four-piece orchestra flooding out to make the evening absolutely perfect. The men are dressed in their military-style, mess dress; the ladies looking the part in their evening gowns.

It's a long way to come for a pitman's lad – a long way to come for a couple of secondary school kids in just eighteen years. Hand in hand, my wife and I can't help but reflect what our shoeless parents of the 1920's would make of it all.

But not thirty miles away, London is burning. Race riots are spreading out to engulf major cities throughout the country. Yet we're here, in this surreal, summer palace of music, swishing gowns and breathing in rose scented air.

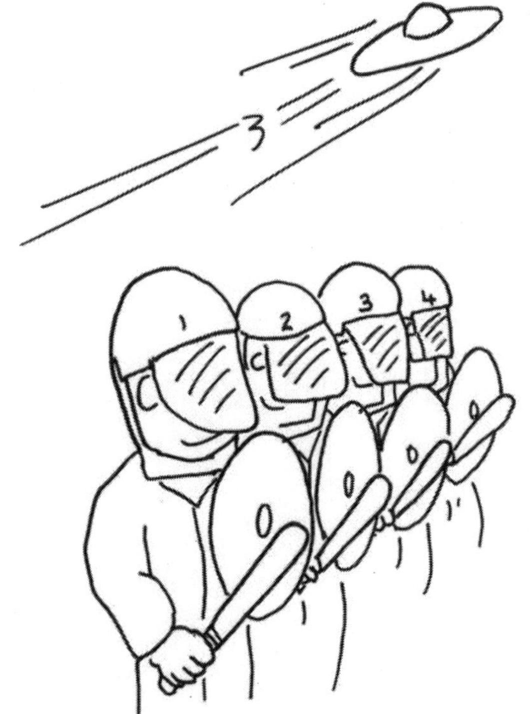

Although I still had many years to serve, I could feel my career coming to an end. A premonition if you like. Earlier in the day, I'd watched in horror as the police service I knew, became an unrecognizable force.

Our instructor hadn't turned up, so our class of fifteen strong-willed individuals destined for life at the top, went walk-about. Something was going on.

What was 'going on' was a demonstration of things to come. Police vans with the by now familiar wire mesh cage covering the windscreen, came hurtling onto the parade ground. Out of the back doors came alien beings – creatures covered from head to toe in black, fire retardant clothing, jack boots, black crash helmets with visors, gauntlets: Aliens or Storm Troopers who carried shields and long batons. They form up, long lines of faceless men, all beating their shields in an unnerving rhythm.

They certainly frightened me.

But it wasn't the race riots they were practising or preparing for. No! This was a sign of things to come. It was for the Miners in 1984; Maggie's infamous, "Enemy within."

It had taken a couple of decades, but the police had changed from the 'Heartbeat' days – the days of the Thick Blue Line to…..

And that's the problem. I don't think anyone knows any more.